War
and
Peace

War and Peace

from Genesis to Revelation

King Jesus' Manual of Arms for the 'Armless

Vernard Eller

A Christian Peace Shelf Selection

Wipf and Stock Publishers

EUGENE, OREGON

Wipf and Stock Publishers
199 West 8th Avenue, Suite 3
Eugene, Oregon 97401
ISBN-13: 978-1-5326-6626-1
War and Peace
From Genesis to Revelation
By Eller, Vernard
Copyright© January, 1981 Herald Press

Publication date: May, 2003 .
Previously published by Herald Press, January, 1981 .

In homage to

The King

in whose service the work was wrought
and to whose cause it is dedicated

Contents

Preface to the Revised Edition

The Christian Peace Shelf board asked me to prepare this newly revised edition of my 1973 Abingdon Press book, *King Jesus' Manual of Arms for the 'Armless: War and Peace from Genesis to Revelation*—this out of a feeling that my biblical study was still relevant and worthy of attention for a new decade. Of course I concurred with that judgment and welcomed it. (The Christian Peace Shelf is a joint effort of Herald Press and a Mennonite Central Committee Peace Section advisory board with representation from the Brethren in Christ Church, the General Conference Mennonite Church, the Mennonite Brethren Church, and the Mennonite Church. For a listing of Christian Peace shelf selections, see page 219 of this book.)

My first move, consequently, was to excise those references that dated the book to the Vietnam era; as it now stands, it is oriented solely to the Scriptures and is equally applicable at any time, to any situation. I also made a number of stylistic changes in the interest of appealing to a broader age-group audience (the intention now being high school through adults).

In the way of new material, a number of scattered sentences and paragraphs have been added; but the major, block additions are two. The first, in Chapter 5, is a crucial argument that, in his public ministry (including his death and resurrection), the historical Jesus of Nazareth did consciously and deliberately set out to practice and fulfill what this book calls the Old Testament Zion/Suffering-Servant Model.

The second addition consists of a number of pages in the final chapter—namely, the entire crusade/crossbearing, secular/eschatological, flatland/round-earth distinction. I consider that this makes the outcome and point of the study much more clear, concrete, and persuasive than it was before. I have also added an index of biblical passages used.

First time around, this book generally speaking was well received both by reviewers and other readers. Indeed, I was taken by surprise when *Publishers Weekly,* the mouthpiece of the secular industry, opined, "Agnostics and skeptics along with the large number of readers among his co-religionists could very well appreciate [Eller's] original ... interpretations." My prayer with this new edition is that the book will continue to attract attention, not particularly to itself, but to the biblical message it is intended to serve.

> *Vernard Eller*
> University of La Verne (CA)
> Fall 1980

Introduction

If there is one biblical prophecy that was fulfilled the moment it was uttered and has been re-fulfilled continuously ever since, it is Jesus' prediction about wars and rumors of war (Mark 13:7-8). Particularly is this so if we understand "wars" to include not only actual military engagements but all sorts of interpersonal violence—and "violence," in turn, to include any activity that *violates* the dignity and God-image of persons, whether physically, verbally, psychologically, socially, economically, spiritually, or in any way whatever. And given this definition, there is no need to go beyond the morning newspaper to document that *war* is and has been the constant state of humanity. But what has the Bible to say about this? Does God have a word that ought to be heard? It is to an effort at finding out that this book is dedicated. But that dedication creates a situation about which I am sorry. It can be said here at the outset that our book is going to be more than a little strange. The reader will need to demonstrate even more than the usual amount of indulgence, trying not to form a judgment until he sees how the whole business comes out. The case is that our study will take off in one direction and wind up headed 180 degrees the other way.

That isn't my fault, and it wasn't my choice or desire. When the decision was made to let the Bible speak its piece, we were bound to go where it chooses to take us; and the way it chooses is

roundabout. Now the *shortest* distance between two points may
be a straight line, but the *best* way of getting from one to the
other may not be. To read the Bible requires *faith*. And part of
that faith is the trust that the Bible knows where it is going even
when it heads north in order to go south.

Like the first, there is also a second aspect of the matter
which calls for our indulgence. As we shall discover, the way of
the Lord does indeed lead into paths of *peace*. Nevertheless, the
marking of the route is done at every point in the images and
metaphors of *militarism*. The language is that of war; the content
is that of peace. Those whose peaceable sensibilities are such that
they get uptight over the use of military imagery will not be able
to appropriate the Bible's teaching *against* war, for it is couched
almost entirely in the terminology *of* war.

The plan is to begin with Genesis and plow straight through
to Revelation. But rest assured, the book won't be all that long.
We will not feel obliged to examine each and every verse that
speaks of war and rumors of war, peace and rumors of peace. We
will hit only the high points, those benchmark passages that plot
the general development and indicate the crucial turning points
of the biblical position. We will try not to bog down into the jot-
and-tittle nitpicking that Bible study sometimes becomes.

In preparation for writing the book I have done considerable
study in the works of biblical scholars; but I will keep that
between me and them. It is not that they have failed to be helpful; quite the contrary, without their findings the book could
never have been written. Nevertheless, they will be kept behind
the scenes. We are resisting the temptation to become technical
and difficult.

What we shall discover is that the Bible as a whole presents a
unified argument regarding peace and war. By "unified argument" we do not mean to suggest that a person would find the Bible saying *the same thing* about peace and war no matter where
he happened to dip in. That obviously is not the case. We do not
mean to suggest that the teachings of Joshua, commander of the

conquest of the Promised Land, are the same as those of Jesus (whose name is actually but a variant of "Joshua"), conqueror of sin, death, and the devil.

However, we *do* mean to say that the case is *not* as it customarily is presented, as though the Bible reverses its field somewhere between Joshua and Jesus, as though accepting Jesus necessarily entails the renunciation of Joshua. Not at all. We will find that there is a very clear and logical chain of thought from one to the other, a completely consistent development.

"Unified argument" means, then, that each step, each new development, picks up what has gone before, reinterprets and re-fashions it at points, but also assimilates it into the new position which then is passed on to the next station in line. This continuity will add real interest and power to our study; but it also means that we will need again to practice that indulgence which withholds judgment until Jesus has an opportunity to tell us what was the true significance of Joshua.

Finally, as it may turn out to our joy or to our chagrin, we are going to discover that the Bible has some rather strong admonishment to deliver both to the war advocates and the peace advocates in our midst. Again, the reader will have to stick with us for quite awhile—perhaps to the very end of the book—before all this comes clear; but that's how it has to be.

War and Peace

1
Wherefrom
Do They Come?

*From whence come wars and fightings among you? come they not hence,
even of your lusts that war in your members? Ye lust, and have not: ye kill,
and desire to have, and cannot obtain: ye fight and war, yet ye have not, because ye ask not. Ye ask, and receive not, because ye ask amiss, that ye may
consume it upon your lusts.*

—James 4:1-3, KJV

It is James, one of the latest writers in the Bible, who asks
concerning the source of wars and fightings. He answers his own
question; but although his answer undoubtedly is *true* enough, it
hardly is *adequate*.

In the first place, no modern would recognize a "lust" if one
bit him, and certainly he would deny that he has them in his
members (whatever "members" may be). And, in the second
place, James's answer stops too soon in failing to tell us where the
lusts come from.

If he were pressed further, he likely would refer us to the
book entitled *Wherefrom* (which is what "Genesis" means); it
tells us where a great many things come from. As we focus upon
the Adam and Eve story, Dietrich Bonhoeffer's little book, *Crea-*

tion and Fall, will be most helpful to us. Beginning with the story of Cain and Abel, Jacques Ellul's *The Meaning of the City* takes the lead.

Wherefrom, then, do they come—these wars and fightings which so everlastingly plague the race called "human"?

Well, "In the beginning, God created . . ."; that's about as far back as we can get.

"But you don't mean to suggest that *this* is where wars and fightings come from: from the fact that God created them into the nature of the heavens and the earth?"

Yes and no—mostly no. But if we are to get an answer to our question, it will be essential to understand that the heavens and the earth, their life and history, were designed by God, put in motion by him toward the end and for the purposes of his own choosing. God has something in mind for his creation and even now is working to bring it about. This is not necessarily to say that anything and everything that subsequently appears is of his desire and doing. It is to say that nothing we do find can be explained *apart from*, or in neglect of, his desire and doing. Besides, if we start with the first verse of the first chapter of the first book of the Bible, no one can accuse us of having skipped over something important in the process of getting started.

> So God created man in his image; in the image of God he created him; male and female he created them. God blessed them and said to them, "Be fruitful and increase, fill the earth and subdue it, rule over the fish in the sea, the birds of heaven, and every living thing that moves upon the earth."
>
> Genesis 1:27-28.

"We are getting closer, I guess; you do have to have men before you can have wars and fightings among men. But do you mean to suggest that God *created* us to be warriors and fighters?"

No and yes—mostly *yes* (how does that grab you?). The key here, obviously, is that man was created in the *image* of God.

"Image" implies some sort of likeness between the Creator and the created one. But what points of likeness does the author have in mind? That's the problem; he doesn't say.

Yet maybe he *does*. The words immediately following would be the logical place to look; what an author says *next* always is the best clue for getting an understanding of what he said *last*. And in this case, the next verse represents God's very first command to the new, image-created man; perhaps the intent is: "If you are going to be in my image, act thus." And notice the verbs in that *thus:* "increase," "fill the earth," "subdue it," "rule." Them's *fightin'* words where I come from! The implication is that to be in "the image of God" means to be a *fighter*.

The matter can be sliced just a bit finer than that. The command to man clearly is that he is to "take charge," "exert control over," "run things." Now these terms do not necessarily amount to wars and fightings—unless somebody or something decides to *resist* such control. But once resistance shows itself, wars and fightings are inevitable. Indeed, "the effort to exert control over that which resists control" would constitute a rather good definition of "wars and fightings."

Notice, however, that, although the verbs of our text suggest very strongly that there is (or will be) resistance, the passage gives absolutely no hint as to what will constitute it or where it will arise. The enemy is not named nor is any instruction given on *how* he is to be fought. Certainly, nothing is said here about man clobbering *other people;* and plainly, the author does not mean to say that man should clobber the lithe little fishies that swim in the sea or those darling darters of song that flit about the heavens. Who or how man is to fight we simply are not told.

However, one aspect of the case follows automatically. If man in the image of God is a fighter, it must be that he is to fight *as* God *fights*. And that God *fights* we have as much as said already. God created with a purpose in mind. He has a plan for his world which he intends should be fulfilled. In one way or another, he has taken charge and is exerting control. If and when any resistance shows itself, there will be a fight.

But that man is to fight *in the image of God* does protect us from one misinterpretation that recently has been foisted upon this text. Some people have gone overboard on *eco*logy in such a way as to imbalance their *theo*logy; they maintain that the biblical teaching about *subduing* the earth and *ruling* nature is the equivalent of inviting us to *misuse* the earth and *exploit* nature. But the command we are considering cannot mean that and does not mean that. Obviously, *God's* control is not aimed at raping, devastating, and perverting the nature he created, but at enhancing it, enriching it, directing it toward the end for which he made it in the first place. His command, then, is that man wage the same fight toward the same end.

The Bible gives that end a name which is the only appropriate one for it. It is not until the New Testament that the *name* comes into view, although the *idea* behind it can be traced clear back here to the creation story. What God is fighting for is the establishment of "the kingdom of God." That conclusion is not too surprising, because the New Testament phrase, "the kingdom of God," means nothing more or less than "the kingly *rule* of God." The Lord's Prayer puts it precisely: "thy kingdom come" is the exact equivalent of "thy will be done on earth." What it comes to, then, is that God is determined to fight, to exert his control, until that control is complete, until all resistance, anything at all contrary to his will, is forever done away. As we said, the matter is obvious: the end toward which God exerts his control is to make his control complete. But what becomes significant—and will remain of prime significance throughout this book—is that, if the man commanded to fight is himself in *the image of God*, then he must fight for the same end, namely, that God's kingly rule might be all in all.

(What we have yet to do is find out where the resistance comes from, who or what takes the role, and how it is to be brought under control. Yet, as regards these questions, our present text is of no help.)

But to fight in the image of God—there is more that must be said. When we think of man in the image of God, in all likelihood we picture God as a big tall one and man as an itty-bitty version of the same thing standing alongside—after the fashion by which one determines that a son is the spittin' image of his father. But this probably is not the most helpful way to think.

The picture here to be suggested is modeled after a movement ballet dancers sometimes make—at least it looks to me as though that is what is going on. My field is theology rather than ballet, and the following must be understood accordingly.

The male dancer and his female partner are facing each other. He raises an arm; she raises her corresponding arm in imitation. He raises his other arm; she raises hers. He spreads a leg sideways; she does too. He pulls the other leg up to it; so does she. And so they dance all over the place, moving in perfect unison as she takes her cue from him, responding in instant obedience, dancing *in his image*.

This would seem to get closer to the truth of the matter than any suggestion that God and man are built alike or that they take identical roles (*to lead* is obviously an entirely different role from *to follow*).

We can push the analogy a bit further. In the dance, for some reason or other, it seems to be the ballerina who really struts her stuff and draws all the attention; and interestingly enough, God himself is not averse to taking the more quiet and invisible role. But even so, the ballerina is completely dependent upon the male dancer. It could be (and let us make it so in our instance) that he is the choreographer as well as her dance partner. Furthermore, many of her didoes are possible only because he actually is supporting, holding, and guiding her so that she *can* do them. In such case, of course, she must put absolute faith and trust in him.

So the God who fights to establish his kingdom creates man in his own image and commands him to fight, too. They are together in the same fight, and their relationship is a very close and intimate one. But it does not follow that man is to be simply a little god. He is fighting to enforce *God's* control, not his own. He is to conduct himself in obedient response to *God's* directives rather than according to his own wisdom and initiative.

At this point we are not yet close to speaking of *peace*. We haven't even made a good start on answering James's question about *war*. For one thing, we haven't been able to locate an enemy. For another, it is plain that the wars James was asking about are not those aimed at the establishing of the kingdom of God. Nevertheless, we now are able to say one very important thing about what biblical "peace" cannot and will not be.

Peace—what the Bible means by "peace"—will not be just a refusal to fight, a claiming exemption from any effort to take charge of creation and exert control over it. Such is in direct contradiction to the primal command given to man.

Some people in our day think to create "peace" by stepping out of man's vocation as ruler *over* nature and fighter *for* nature, simply to merge in as part and parcel *of* nature. For instance, the "flower children" of a generation ago—except when moved to outbursts of rage—idealized "peace" as the state of the flowers themselves, i.e., totally passive, not trying to exert any sort of control, content just to be acted *upon*, to receive whatever comes along.

Now call that state what you will, but don't call it "peace." "Peace" we shall get to in due course; but here at the outset it is made plain that what the Bible means by peace cannot entail man's renunciation of his having been imaged by the fighting God, merely to take refuge in the passive world of nature out of which he was called. Man never was meant to be "at one with nature" in this sense. God, as we shall see, does want men of peace; but he very certainly does *not* want men with all the "fight" taken out of them. The biblical ideal is something quite different.

But we'll never get to James's kind of wars and fightings until we get more people on the scene.

And so the Lord God put the man into a trance, and while he slept, he took one of his ribs and closed the flesh over the place. The Lord God then built up the rib, which he had taken out of the man, into a woman. He brought her to the man, and the man said:

> Now this, at last—
> bone from my bones,
> flesh from my flesh!—
> this shall be called woman,
> for from man was this taken.

> That is why a man leaves his father and mother and is united to his wife, and the two become one flesh.

> Now they were both naked, the man and his wife, but they had no feeling of shame toward one another.
>
> Genesis 2:21-25.

"This is it, then? Wars and fightings come from the fact that there are other people? Where two or three are gathered, there is bound to be a fight?"

NO! The text does not so much as hint at anything of the sort. We still are dealing with man in the image of God, but all the fighting language is gone; there is nothing here about ruling or exerting control over others. In its stead is language to make love by: "bone from my bones," "flesh from my flesh," "united to," "the two become one flesh." I belong to you, because you belong to me. Everything points to a mutual *giving* of oneself to the other—the very contrary of *domination over* the other. Clearly, in creating "the other person," God had no intention of providing man with "the enemy." This is the very *last* place for man to apply his fighting instincts, for this one was created to be *lover*, not *enemy*. The command to fight still stands, but it is not the other person who is to be fought.

The concluding verse makes the situation even more apparent than the earlier verses did. Naked came the stranger, precisely so that it could be seen that *she* wasn't a stranger, that *he* wasn't a stranger. Nothing here to fear; nothing here to hide; nothing here to fight. Only that which belongs; only that which calls forth love. Nothing here, either, which needs to be claimed, possessed, used, exploited, dominated. Such attitudes apply only toward that which does *not* belong to me; but here the nakedness surely is intended as the very symbol of a profound sort of mutuality and belonging. Thus this nakedness has an entirely different significance than the nakedness so flaunted and celebrated among us today. There is no suggestion here of using nakedness as a way of enticing the other person into my power; no suggestion here of getting myself naked in order to use the other person for my own pleasure.

The way our passage falls within the story as a whole would indicate that the author has in mind much more than just a *sexual* relationship. Rather, he is using the man and woman as a model of what, each in its own way, every person-to-person relationship is intended to be. Sex and nakedness (*this sort* of sex and nakedness, it must be said) represent the most intense level of the quality of relationship that should characterize human interaction at *all* levels.

And the point of our first parents' nakedness is that there is *nothing between them*—not so much as a blush of shame. No barriers, no secrets, no regrets, no facades, no intimidation, no status distinctions, no suspicion. The relationship is that of frankness, honesty, trust, openness, "here-I-amness," *nakedness*. "Shame"—which is the condign and involuntary admission that one is in the wrong—is the worst possible thing that could come between them, for it is itself the sign of other deep and serious barriers. But here there is nakedness and yet no shame, absolutely *no* shame. And this, it must be said, is an entirely different phenomenon from the "shamelessness" that marks so much of modern nudity. That shamelessness is the brazen determination to ignore the wrongness that is present; the biblical "naked but unashamed" is a witness to the fact that nothing *is* wrong.

By now, one thing has been made quite plain: it is not the

simple *existence* of the other person that constitutes the wherefrom of James's wars and fightings. The other person is not an inevitable source of contention. Rather, when we are in the image of God as we were created to be, the other person is a source of love, harmony, and belonging that is the highest form of *peace*. Thus, if, by "human nature," we intend that which was created into man from the beginning, then wars and fightings do not arise out of human nature. Human nature, naked and unashamed in the presence of another, produces peace. But as we shall discover, it is man's "inhuman nature" that leads to war. The other person is not, either by nature or by necessity, the *enemy*.

> "You may eat from every tree in the garden, but not from the tree of knowledge of good and evil; for on the day that you eat from it, you will certainly die." . . . The serpent said, "Of course you will not die. God knows that as soon as you eat it, your eyes will be opened and you will be *like God* knowing both good and evil." When the woman saw that the fruit of the tree was good to eat, and that it was pleasing to the eye and tempting to contemplate, she took some and ate it. She also gave her husband some and he ate it.
>
> Genesis 2:16-17 and 3:4-6; italics mine.

Clearly, the Bible wants to tell us that something of critical importance happened when man (the man and the woman in collusion, without any distinction as to guilt) ate from the forbidden tree. Once we understand what it was that occurred, we will have the answer to James's question.

Why did man eat that which God did not want him to eat? What did he hope to get out of it? The serpent puts it perfectly, "You will be *like God!*"

Now here is something new—something radically and spectacularly new. Man already is "in the image of God," so the possibility of now becoming "like God" must be something entirely different. To be "like God" is to reject the ballet-dancers' model and go to something more akin to the spittin' image model of the father and his little boy.

The ballerina can be "the image" of her partner only as long as he is present and active in the dance—indeed, only as long as he continues to lead and she continues to follow. But the boy is "like" his daddy in that each is an independent being even though they display many common characteristics. The boy can grow up; the daddy can die; and the son can take the father's place—all without in any way violating the concept of being "spittin' image." And it is precisely to this new sort of relationship that the man and woman now aspire; they want to graduate from "image of God" to being "like God."

But why is the fruit of this particular tree the crux of the matter? Well, if Adam is to break his dependency upon God and take over the God-functions for himself, one thing he will have to have is *a knowledge* (of good and evil) *of his own*, a knowledge that he possesses in and of himself, that *he* controls, that he can use for his own purposes. Earlier he had no need for such—any more than, according to our weak analogy, the ballerina needs to know ahead of time what path the dance will take, needs to be able to *decide* what path the dance *should* take. That is not her job; her job is to follow the lead of the partner. However, once she asks her partner to leave the stage so that she can dance *like* he does, this new and different order of knowledge will be an absolute necessity. This, then, is the apple that man *has* to have if there is to be any chance of his being "like God."

There is nothing here, of course, to suggest that before this time man had *no* knowledge or was not expected to use his head. It takes a pretty smart cookie to be a ballerina; and man has plenty of room to exercise all of his mind and abilities just in discovering the will of God and doing it. God has given him all signals GO in that direction; there is no prohibition. Man indeed is wonderfully made, including some rather fantastic and sophisticated circuit design and the capability of some very impressive performance. Nevertheless, his circuitry is that of a *receiver* rather than a *transmitter*—and nothing can change the fact.

But man couldn't be content with that; he had to eat the apple and become *like* God. But what he discovered was that, having eaten the apple, he wasn't man enough (better, wasn't *God* enough) to digest it; his system wasn't built to take it. So he came down with a bellyache like you wouldn't believe. Indeed *as a dancer*, he was *dead*—because he had refused the ballerina role that he *could* handle. And because each of us has felt it necessary to repeat the Adam trick for ourselves, that deathdealing bellyache has persisted right down to the present day.

But how does this change of role affect the fight that the God-imaged man had been commissioned to wage? Well, if it had been fought by dancing to God's lead, it would, naturally, have been God's fight, fought for his end (the kingdom of God), against the enemy he designated, and according to his strategies. As we shall see, the new Adam continues to be a fighter—oh, a *very* good fighter, one of the best. But, fought with apple-knowledge, the fight is now for his own end (the kingdom of the new god, Adam), against enemies and according to strategies of his own choosing. The only difficulty with this is that it regularly turns out to be the wrong war, fought against the wrong adversaries in the wrong way at the wrong place.

> Then the eyes of both of them were opened and they discovered that they were naked; so they stitched fig leaves together and made themselves loincloths. The man and his wife heard the sound of the Lord God walking in the garden at the time of the evening breeze and hid from the Lord God among the trees of the garden. But the Lord God called to the man and said to him, "Where are you?" He replied, "I heard the sound as you were walking in the garden, and I was afraid because I was naked, and I hid myself." God answered, "Who told you that you were naked? Have you eaten from the tree which I forbade you?" The man said, "The woman you gave me for a companion, she gave me fruit from the tree and I ate it."
>
> Genesis 3:7-12.

You were inquiring about wars and fightings? Behold, they come—with a vengeance.

"Eat the fruit," the serpent had said, "and your eyes will be opened." So the man ate, his eyes *were* opened, and what did he see? The other side of his God-like mounting; he saw that he was NAKED. There was an instant convulsion of arms, legs, elbows and hands in an attempt to cover up and a frantic snatching for leaves; it would have been something to see. The case would seem to be that it was not the nudity of the other person that was found so shocking; it was the looking down at one's own threadbare and bare-of-threads self.

On a God-imaged human being, nudity had looked good. As garb for a God-like god, this new emperor's clothes were just too transparent. Man suddenly saw that he doesn't have what it takes for his new office; there was nothing to do but cover up in an effort to hide the fact. Gone was the frankness, honesty, trust, openness, the "here-I-amness," the God-pleasing, man-pleasing nakedness of yore. In had come *shame;* and with shame, up go the barriers. Shame, too, we should note, is one very good source for Jamesian wars and fightings: take out after the other person's wrongness in order to divert attention from your own.

God comes. Man hides. Man *hiding* from God? The ballerina *afraid* of the one through whom she is a dancer? How strange things have become! But *fear,* too, is a good wherefrom for wars and fightings; lash out at the shadows that menace!

"The woman you gave me for a companion, she gave me fruit." Catch that. Not fifteen verses earlier she had been "bone of my bones," "flesh of my flesh," the one with whom I have become one. Now suddenly she has turned into that blankety-blank woman *you* foisted on me, Lord. I'm not to blame for what happened; *you* created her!

One might get the impression that, for Adam, things are rather falling apart; he bears all the marks of a desperate man, trying to *placate* God but *arousing* his wife in the process—a very poor move. And here, by the way, is one of the best of all sources for wars and fightings: the making of disparaging remarks about one's dutiful and loving wife.

With that, we return to a prior question: Do wars and fightings arise from the fact that man was created the way he was? NO: if man had remained in the image of God as he should have, there never would have been any wars and fightings of the Jamesian variety. YES: it is *because* man was created in the image of God that he had the *possibility* of making the choice that led inevitably to wars and fightings. You see, part of what it means to be in the image of God is that one is able to follow the lead of God freely, voluntarily, by choice. It would be no good dance if the ballerina were *tied* to her partner, a dummy whose moves in actuality are propelled by the partner. No, the marvel of the dance is precisely that they are altogether *her* moves *and yet* in complete correspondence to *his* lead. And if you don't think it is a fine art to dance so with God, just try it sometime.

But if man is to be free to dance, he must also be free to *refuse* to dance. That is a risk God had to take; he *had* to make man so; for if there was to be the possibility of dance, there had also to be the possibility of such things as wars and fightings. So God took the risk and was betrayed—even though the resultant wars and fightings in no sense are his doing. But the risk was the right one to take in any case, because it isn't as though God has lost it for good; the bout isn't over yet. God is still in the picture; and it is way too early yet to say that everything has come to nothing.

> The Lord God made tunics of skins for Adam and his wife and clothed them.
> Genesis 3:21.

This may be the most significant verse in the whole story, and yet it is one that customarily gets overlooked. There is here a strange and wonderful thing. God has created Adam in his own image, as perfect man; he has stood by to give him leadership and provide for his every need; he has conferred upon him the benediction of nakedness without shame, the sign of absolute rightness. In return, Adam has told God to drop dead: "I'll dance it by

myself." God, who has respect for man's freedom and is not about
to push in where he isn't wanted, did step back (and Adam fell
flat on his face). Yet God, the fighter God, did not drop dead
(even though some modern Adams would claim otherwise).
Respect for man's freedom does not mean that God has to do
everything man tells him to; God has *some* freedom of his own.

But now, without the anointment of God, man's nakedness
turns to burning shame, a plague under which he cannot live.
Without the anointment of God—which man had rejected and
still rejects—there is no cure; the best that can be done is to cover
up and hide the scald. So who kneels to drape man in the clothing
he never in this world should have needed? I'll tell you who; the
rejected God does, that's who! Would you ever have believed it?

But why? What possible obligation could God have toward
the man who wished him dead, who insisted on going it alone and
now is getting just what he asked for? The obligation of *love* is
what it is. Remember that this God is the father of the one who,
on a cross, prayed, "Father, forgive them, for they know not what
they do"—and did so fully confident that that was just what he
would do—he had done it so many times already.

But remember, too, that this God is a *fighter* who has determined to bring in his kingdom, to make his control of the situation complete. Thus, God isn't about to let man take the full consequences of what he has brought upon himself; they would wipe
him out, and then who would there be to dance with? So what
does God do but sneak in some clothes and a bunch of other blessings that will cushion the shock and keep man on his feet while he
is fighting *against* God so that, when comes the day that he gives
it up as a bad scene and decides to become a ballerina again, there
will still be enough of him left to do it. Now that is a pretty un-
derhanded way of fighting, you must admit. But it's effective. You
bet your life it is (in fact, there is no other bet on which your life
has any chance at all)!

But do you see what all this proves? It proves that MAN IS
NOT THE ENEMY. Man may be the traitor; he most assuredly

is. It may be man's fault that there has to be a fight; that's most assuredly the case. Man may fight against God; he most assuredly does. But God does not fight against man; man is not the enemy. God may fight against that within man which makes him resist love and leading, fight against his lusts (his self-assertive, go-it-alone propensities) which lead to wars and fightings and all manner of anti-God behavior; it is most certain that he does. But in all this, God is fighting *for* man, not against him. God is trying to gain the sort of control that will wrest man free from the chains he has forged for himself and bring him into his true humanity. The enemy is *in* man, but man is not the enemy.

However, with God in the fight, there is not the slightest doubt but that the enemy will be destroyed, that the victory will be God's. And that victory—marked by the elimination of shame and fear and disparaging remarks about dutiful and loving wives, by the elimination of the wars and fightings that spring therefrom—that victory will be PEACE. And the song of peace will be "Dance, Ballerina, Dance."

But all that is *God's* war; and until the victory is his, we still have our own Jamesian wars with which to contend. On them we hardly have started.

> Cain said to his brother Abel, "Let us go into the open country." While they were there, Cain attacked his brother Abel and murdered him. Then the Lord said to Cain, "Where is your brother Abel?" Cain answered "I do not know. Am I my brother's keeper?" The Lord said, "What have you done? Hark! your brother's blood that has been shed is crying out to me from the ground. Now you are accursed, and banished.... You shall be a vagrant and a wanderer on earth." ... Then Cain went out from the Lord's presence and settled in the land of Nod to the east of Eden.... Cain was then building a city, which he named Enoch.
> Genesis 4:8-11, 13, 16-17.

Genesis does not stop with questions of "wherefrom do they come" but proceeds to "whereto do they go." And regarding wars

and fightings, the "whereto" word of Genesis is a word of our day:
ESCALATION.

What, in the first generation, showed itself in a disparaging
remark about a dutiful and loving wife and a grab for cover, in the
very next generation becomes brother slaughtering brother, a
man laid out with the cover pulled clear up over his face. We
often attribute war to population pressures and all like that; but it
sure didn't take much in the way of population to start the ball
rolling in the first place.

Yet what is even more chilling than the sight of Abel dead in
his blood is Cain's answer to the inquiry, "Where is your
brother?": "How should I know? I don't take any responsibility
for *him*." We are talking about two *persons*, two God-imaged
men created to be "bone of my bone," "flesh of my flesh," two
who have become one. Now, one of these men totally disclaims
any knowledge of or concern over the other: "For me, he doesn't
exist." This sort of *indifference* is a whole order worse than hate,
violence, or murder; those qualities at least are personal enough to
recognize the other's existence so as to have at him.

Adam had broken his "image" relationship *with* God in
order to go it alone *like* God. How totally devastating was that
breach becomes apparent only here when the lone Cain denies
that he even *has* a brother.

And this, my friends, is the name of war: the denial that I
even *have* a brother.

Comes, then, the consequence, the flight of Cain: "accursed," "banished," "a vagrant and a wanderer," "out from the
Lord's presence," "in the land of *Nod* [which means, Wander-
ing]," "east of Eden [i.e., in the desert far, far away from home]."
Put it all together, it spells INSECURITY. And this catches *us*; it
describes *our* state. For consider that we are all children of Cain;
Abel was cut off, leaving no descendants. And the land of Nod is
not dreamland, as we fain would have it. It is *here*, the place of
our insecurity and our wandering; it is us, vagrant, *away* from the
presence of the Lord.

Insecurity is both a cause and a fruit of war. To be in the image of God is itself a *secure* position; the presence and guidance of the Partner gives the ballerina a center and a home. But to go it alone, *like* God, is to be thrown completely upon my own resources—which means precisely the *lack* of security. And with this, the race begins to splinter. Frightened in my insecurity, I become jealous of the brother who seems to have it made. I wipe him out. Then I really am insecure. The guilt and shame of what I have done put me to flight—and my direction is *east*, away even from whatever security I *had* known. This, for us sons of Cain, is wherefrom our wars and fightings come and whereto they go.

But Cain *has* to do *something*; the life of ceaseless, easeless wandering is unbearable. He *builds* a city, the first such mentioned in the Bible (note well *who* built it, *why* he built it, and *where* he built it). Cain built it in the land of Nod as an attempt to create security for himself. But "create" is the wrong word in that sentence; its Hebrew equivalent is *reshith*, the word used to identify *God's* activity in Genesis 1:1. But Cain's city is named Enoch *(chanakh)*, which means "to initiate" or "to inaugurate"; it indicates man's effort to start something on his own for himself.

Cain tries to build, to manufacture, SECURITY. The biblical writer undoubtedly thinks of the city Enoch as a walled fortress, complete with munitions factories, armories, and Pentagons. War does tend to be a city-based activity, you know. Now "security" has acquired precisely the connotations it has in modern government vocabulary: when we say "security," we mean *guns*. And like his, *ours* is the wrongheaded, misguided, self-defeating, banished, and accursed "security" of Cain crouched in Enoch.

"'My brother? How should I know?'" snarls Cain, the blood dripping from his hands. Where will it all lead? Through Genesis and beyond, it will lead from murder to murder, until one day, in the land of Nod, the sons of Cain gang up to do in another brother, this one the Son of God. Yet that death finally will turn things around and get them headed back *west*—*toward* Eden. But that's another chapter.

Lamech said to his wives:
 "Adah and Zillah, listen to me;
 wives of Lamech, mark what I say:
 I kill a man for wounding me,
 a young man for a blow.
 Cain may be avenged seven times,
 but Lamech seventy-seven."

Genesis 4:23-24.

Escalation. "One tough hombre" has appeared on the scene—
and him we will always have with us. Undoubtedly it is the fact
that he had *two* wives that made him that way—a fine source for
wars and fightings. Oh, how we need the one who will turn that
seven-to-seventy-seven ratio from vengeance to forgiveness!

When Noah woke from his drunken sleep, he learnt what his young-
est son had done to him [namely, spread the word that Daddy was
dead drunk and stark naked, a sorry sight either way], and said:

 "Cursed be Canaan,
 slave of slaves
 shall he be to his brothers."

Genesis 9:24-25.

Escalation. The old man makes a fool of himself—and then gets
mad at the person who discovers it, as though *he* were the one
who had caused the trouble. A father cursing his son for what the
father himself had done and damning the boy to a position of
slavery—that is what you might call "a generation gap," another
beautiful source for wars and fightings.

Nimrod ... began to show himself a man of might on earth; and he
was a mighty hunter before the Lord, as the saying goes, "Like
Nimrod, a mighty hunter before the Lord." His kingdom in the beginning, consisted of Babel, Erech, and Accad, all of them in the
land of Shinar. From that land he migrated to Asshur and built
Nineveh, Rehoboth-Ir, Calah, and Resen.

Genesis 10:8-12.

Escalation. Here we have Nimrod, "a man of might on earth."
Jacques Ellul suggests that the Hebrew could be, and probably
should be, translated as "a mighty conqueror on whom the Lord
kept a close eye" rather than "a mighty hunter before the Lord."

It makes better sense; the lines following that one speak only
of city-building, an activity that is not particularly appropriate to
Nimrod's identification as a "hunter." Builder (or taker) of cities,
leader of man's "*security* forces," undoubtedly they called him
"Old Blood and Guts." It is good to have the note, though, that
God was keeping an eye on him. As we marvel at mighty men like
Nimrod, it is difficult sometimes to recall that God is still around.

Nimrod's territory, it goes without saying, lies within the
land of Nod; but his particular fief is called *Shinar,* i.e., "he who
throws down, the shaker, the sign of fury and roaring." One of the
cities within that realm is Babel; we'll get to it in a bit. And within
the area of his new conquests stands Nineveh, which, for the Old
Testament, comes to be *the* city of cruel, bloodthirsty, rapacious
WAR. "As the saying goes, 'Like Nimrod, a mighty conqueror on
whom the Lord kept a close eye.' "

Escalation. From Adam to Cain to Lamech to Noah to
Nimrod the line goes; and with each step it comes nearer to *us.*

> Once upon a time all the world spoke a single language and used
> the same words. As men journeyed in the east, they came upon a
> plain in the land of Shinar and settled there.... "Come," they said,
> "let us build ourselves a city and a tower with its top in the heavens,
> and make a name for ourselves; or we shall be dispersed all over the
> earth." Then the Lord came down to see the city and tower which
> mortal men had built, and he said, "Here they are, one people with
> a single language, and now they have started to do this; hencefor-
> ward nothing they have a mind to do will be beyond their reach.
> Come, let us go down there and confuse their speech, so that they
> will not understand what they say to one another." So the Lord dis-
> persed them from there all over the earth, and they left off building
> the city. That is why it is called Babel, because the Lord made a
> babble of the language of all the world.
>
> Genesis 11:1-2, 4-9.

Continuing to move *east* (away from the presence of the
Lord), in the land of *Shinar*, the sons of *Nimrod* decide that they
are going to build themselves a city to end all cities. "This one will
really make us secure! It's going to have a tower that will punch
us through to heaven. [It never got *quite* that high. The text says
that God had to 'come down' even to see the thing.] And we'll
make a name for ourselves!"

Here, on a grand scale, is a bald attempt to become *like* God.
And obviously, if man *could* pull it off, he finally would be *secure*.
But God came down to put an end to the whole heroic effort.
Why? Was he afraid that man might succeed and thus make God
himself superfluous? I think not. Was it punishment for insubordi-
nation, then? No, not even that. Rather: "These people are getting skilled and powerful enough that they actually are going to
try some of the wild-eyed schemes they dream up. If someone
doesn't step in, they are very likely to kill their fool selves."

God's cutting of the communication lines is of a piece with
his sewing garments of skins to clothe them—a rather sly way of
protecting man from himself until such time as God can get him
straightened out. And on Pentecost, by the way, God *did* recon-
nect those lines.

So this is the way it goes with us. Let us build high, higher,
higher, the ancient sacrifice: the human race torn all apart. And
now, in the city of Babel (my city, your city, our city) the race is
torn so completely apart that brother no longer can communicate
with brother, even if he should decide he wants to.

Meanwhile, back in the Garden sits God, sewing tunics.
Compared to Nimrodian conquests and Babylonian tower-build-
ing that doesn't seem like much; but it is going to win the day—
indeed it will!

That is Genesis on the wherefroms and wheretos of wars and
fightings; with Chapter 12, the focus shifts to the story of God's
efforts to rectify matters.

But does the analysis of the wherefrom of *war* tell us anything helpful about the how-to of *peace*? It does.

If Genesis is correct, then essentially war is a *theological* problem—one centering upon man's relationship to God—rather than a political or sociological one. And if the problem is theological, then ultimately the answer is going to have to be, too. Now certainly, wars and fightings *do* have political and sociological ramifications. And no one is suggesting that we ought not to do what can be done on these levels. Just because we are a race of Nimrods does not mean that, at every point, we have to be the most stupid Nimrods possible. Whenever, for example, we can get our Nimrods quieted a bit, or spending less money, that is worth doing.

Nevertheless, political and social action does not and never will get to the heart of the matter. There never will be *real* peace (although, hopefully, there will be the cessation of *some* hostilities) until man gets away from wanting to be "like God" and is restored to his true status as ballerina. And of course, there is no possible political or social program that can get at this one.

Now by virtue of the fact that ours is a *biblical* study, this book approaches the war problem from the angle of how man is to be restored to that relationship with God which by nature means "peace." This, we claim, is to cut in at a more fundamental and ultimately more promising level than if we were to try to outline programs and techniques of social and political action. This is not to deny the legitimacy of these; but the truth of those studies will need to be measured against the truth of this one, rather than vice versa. That is to say, one ought to make his political actions consistent with his theology rather than the other way around.

And the fact of the matter is that many more books have been written and much more work done regarding the politics and sociology of peace than ever has been done on the theology of peace. There is no need to apologize—and this book does not—for the fact that it is what it is rather than being something else.

There is another important implication that follows from our study thus far. Genesis makes it plain that our wars and fightings

spring from a disrelationship that is so pervasive and endemic to
the race that there is no way—absolutely no way—that man can
correct it on his own. He *can't* go home again; he has neither the
wit, the will, nor the wherewithal to make the turn-around. All
ruts run *east*.

Besides, there is the consideration that it was *God* who was
affronted as the relationship was broken, so he will have to be the
one to say whether he even *wants* it reestablished. But in any case,
there is no chance of man solving the problem of wars and fightings for himself; only God can do it.

It does not follow, however, that we have no alternative but
to wait for him to act. The word is that he has acted, is acting, and
will continue to act—precisely that our problem might be cared
for. With the taking up of the needle, clear back in the Garden, he
declared that he *wanted* the relationship restored and was willing
to live down his hurt in order to make it happen. Furthermore, he
has come and is coming after man in order to get him turned
around and headed *west* toward home.

This means that, although man cannot stop war and create
peace, there is that which he can and should do that peace might
come: he can *let* God work, *cooperate* with God's work, *help* God
in his work. In short, man can begin to learn the ballerina role
again. *How* God teaches and *how* man is to dance, it will take us
the remainder of the book to discover.

2
Hell Is Holy?

War is HELL!
— General of the Armies William Sherman

I know war as few other men now living know it, and nothing to me is more revolting.
— General of the Armies Douglas MacArthur

The Lord is a man of war: Yahweh is his name . . . .
  Thy right hand, O Yahweh, hath dashed in pieces the enemy.
And in the greatness of thine excellency thou hast overthrown them that
  rose up against thee:
Thou sentest forth thy wrath, which consumed them as stubble.
— Moses (Exodus 15:3, 6-7, KJV)

This chapter focuses on the books of Joshua and Judges, with some side glances at other books fore and aft. The main thesis of the material, we shall discover, is precisely as stated in the headnote: "Yahweh is a man of war." (*Yahweh*, by the way, is the name by which the early Hebrews regularly identified their God. Wherever, in our English translations of the Old Testament, the word "LORD" appears, the original read "Yahweh." We will use the name consistently from here on.)

Most modern Christians find Joshua's warrior-God so abhorrent and (as they think) so out of harmony with Jesus and his ideas on the subject that they try to keep Joshua and company out of the picture. The standard ploys are simply to turn the pages very fast and in thick bunches through that part of the Bible; or to explain that the thought represented there is an aberration which is quite extraneous to the real message of the Bible; or to go through a now-you-see-it-now-you-don't sort of exegesis that explains away the obvious meaning of what these texts say.

But thus to evade facing up to Joshua is a very poor strategy that inevitably gets one into the wrong position for facing up to Jesus. Besides, it is a less than honest way of listening to the Bible. Our choice, then, is to "grasp the nettle"—an old phrase suggesting that, when handling the prickly, it will hurt less to grab it with a firm grip than to be cautious and gingerly. And in this case, the advice is right.

This is not to suggest that Joshua and his colleagues are the fountainhead of all truth. If Joshua represented perfect truth and understanding, we would have had no need of Jesus. It should be expected that, as we work our way through the Bible and the history it represents, we will find God being able to get through with some clarifications and insights that man had missed in earlier lessons. *Regarding some aspects of the matter*, it undoubtedly is correct that we see more clearly than Joshua did. But (and this is the more important point) as regards overall orientation and basic presuppositions, Joshua is on the mark and we tend to be a way off it. Further, it simply is not true that Joshua represents an aberration from the greater part of the Bible. Rather, his stance is fundamental to the rest of the Bible, clear through Revelation. More, Jesus *takes for granted* the position of Joshua as the basis for his own witness and teaching; we cannot fully understand Jesus without giving attention to Joshua and his doings.

What it comes to is that Joshua and company had a true perception regarding war and peace but misapplied it (and it takes the remainder of the Bible and Jesus to get that matter straightened out); but we don't even have the true perception. Joshua's is not the *last* word; but his is the only *first* word that has any chance of ever getting us to the last word.

What we will discover from Joshua is this: We usually work under the assumption that the way to get peace is to stop people from fighting. Joshua knows that that one isn't going to happen and *shouldn't*. The move, rather, is to get people to switch from fighting *their* wars to join Yahweh in fighting *his* war.

The difference is this: *Our* wars (including our anti-war wars, or what commonly is known as the "peace" movement) are *Nimrodian* in character. That is, they take place in the city of Babel, state of Shinar, land of Nod. Their track is eastward from Eden, *away* from the presence of the Lord. They represent man's attempt to build security for himself—and the security of *peace*, it must be said, for ultimately this is what both the militarists and the pacifists are after. But in either case, it is to be done "like God," by means of our own wisdom, power, and piety. Of course, our pro-war hawks and our anti-war doves diverge completely in their opinions as to *how* man should go about building this security of peace; but in comparison to Joshua, they would seem to be in complete agreement as to the Nimrodian character of the task.

This brings us to a note which needs to be inserted somewhere and just as well here as later. In the following, some indictments will be brought (by the Bible, I hope, rather than simply by myself) that hit the anti-war warriors as much as they do the pro-war warriors. This is bound to offend some peace people—who, I would guess, are most likely to be the readers picking up this book. I am sorry if things happen this way, but there is no help for it.

Above all, I hope that such readers will not turn away criticism in a way that has become quite common with the movement, namely, in justifying their own actions by pointing out how much worse are those of the pro-war establishment. That is a coward's dodge. It was tried first in the Garden, when Adam attempted to duck out of his own responsibility by shifting the blame to Eve. God, you will recall, didn't buy that one for a minute. It is not enough simply to be more righteous than one's opponent; the greater enormity of his evil does not excuse yours. The will of God is the standard; so face the judgment there, and let the pro-war establishment face it for itself.

Further, there will be some indictments to which I can guess the response: "But I know a great many peace people to whom that does not apply at all." True; but these are not intended as *blanket* indictments. It undoubtedly is the case that those leveled against the pro-war establishment do not apply universally there, either. But our task is not that of being *defensive* by counting the numbers of those to whom it does *not* apply. It is ours to let the Scriptures search us to find the degree and the places to which it *does* apply.

Finally, our critique of the "peace" movement—accompanying that of the "war" movement—is not to indicate that no distinction can be seen between the two. *If* these two parties, so conspicuous on the current scene, were the only alternatives, I, for one, would have absolutely no hesitancy as to which to join; I would be with the peace people—even those I am here free in criticizing. But a major purpose of this book is to show that the Bible presents an alternative that is different from *either* of these other two. It is very important, then, that we let Joshua and the others strike both ways. The strength and uniqueness of the Bible, in this as in many other instances, is that it does not provide the wherewithal for one worldly party to justify itself over against another. Rather, it judges every worldly party in light of a truth, the truth of God, that stands superior to any and all alignments of the world. (Here endeth the note.)

Over against the Nimrodian wars, the wars of *man*—of which we were speaking—stands the war of Yahweh, the war fought for his purposes, in his way, at the time and place and against the enemy of his choosing. Man's role in *this* war, obviously, will be that of a ballerina rather than a Nimrod.

What we are going to find in Joshua and his successors, then, is an absolutely sincere, conscientious, devoted attempt to fight the war of Yahweh in the ballerina mode. Sad to say, the understanding of these people was flawed on some points, and their grand attempt failed. But let it be said in deepest seriousness that, until we are ready once again to try the experiment of Joshua, there is *no* hope that the peace that God intends ever can become a reality. Nimrodian wars of whatever mode simply won't do it.

As we come now to let the Bible itself speak, we have chosen to let three different stories—one from the book of Joshua and two from Judges—do the talking. We will retell and summarize the three in turn so as to have them freshly in mind and then will analyze them together in parallel. The scholarship behind our study is predominantly that of the noted Old Testament scholar, Gerhard von Rad—although the use we will make of the findings is not his doing.

Joshua at Jericho

The children of Israel, freed from Egyptian slavery, were headed for the Promised Land. They got bogged down in the desert for forty years but then made their way north and were gathered on the far side of the Jordan River, ready to strike across and make entrance into Canaan proper. It was evident that the first population center they would encounter, and thus the site of their first major engagement, would be the city of Jericho.

Moses, now, had died, and his successor, Joshua, was in command. He sent out a couple of spies who inveigled themselves into the city, there made contact with the harlot Rahab, and learned what they needed to know. Joshua raised an army and led it across the river—which conveniently dried up to make that possible. Then, at the command of Yahweh, the forces advanced to Jericho, where they were instructed:

> You shall march round the city with all your fighting men, making the circuit of it once, for six days running. Seven priests shall go in front of the Ark carrying seven trumpets made from rams' horns. On

the seventh day you shall march round the city seven times and the priests shall blow their trumpets. At the blast of the rams' horns, when you hear the trumpet sound, the whole army shall raise a great shout; the wall of the city will collapse and the army shall advance, every man straight ahead.

Joshua 6:3-5.

And that is just what happened. The city was completely destroyed and then burnt for good measure.

(Along with this story we shall also use some material from the concluding chapters of Joshua, which constitute a farewell speech in which Joshua reviews the events that had taken place under his leadership.)

Deborah, Barak, and Sisera

(This story is of particular interest. In Judges 4, it is told as part of the historical narrative, written down, undoubtedly, long after the events themselves had transpired. Judges 5, however, is a *poem* recounting the same story. Scholars agree that it probably dates back close to the events themselves and represents some of the earliest material to get incorporated into the Bible. It commonly is referred to as "The Song of Deborah.")

Under Joshua, the Israelites had won a foothold in the land, but, at the time of this story, they were being given a very hard time by the native Canaanites. One of the tribal leaders, a woman named Deborah, was looked to in the crisis. She appointed a man named Barak as her army commander, issued a call, and raised a force of ten thousand men from among the various tribes.

These gathered on Mt. Tabor, a peak that stands alone in the middle of an alluvial plain drained by the River Kishon. The plain was then occupied by a vastly superior Canaanite force, including nine hundred horse-drawn chariots. Sisera was the commander of these Canaanite armies. He made no attempt to attack the mountain hideout. He didn't have to. The Israelites would have to come down sometime, and on the plain his chariots could go into action with victory assured.

But before that happened, there came on a horrendous rainstorm. The Kishon flooded, and the whole plain became a gooey mess. With this, the Israelite guerrillas came howling down the mountain. The Canaanite chariots were in to their axles, the Canaanite horses were slopping around helplessly, the Canaanite soldiers were in panic, and the Canaanite commander deserted his men and took off for home on foot.

He found refuge in the tent of a woman named Jael. She gave him a drink (which may have contained a sleeping potion) and put him to bed. When he was far gone, she proceeded to make him all gone by putting a tent peg in his ear and driving it on through, pinning him to the floor.

Gideon and the Midianites
The time is later. The troublemakers are the Midianites. The Israelite organizer is Gideon. He sends out a call to arms and gets thirty-two thousand volunteers. When he invites anyone who would rather not fight to leave, twenty-two thousand go home. Using an arbitrary little water-drinking test, Gideon cuts the remaining ten thousand down to three hundred and goes with that.

As any smart commander would, he outfitted his men with jars and trumpets and torches and swords; and they sneaked up on enemy armies that "lay there in the valley like a swarm of locusts; there was no counting their camels; in number they were like grains of sand on the seashore" (Judges 7:12).

In the middle of the night, then, on signal, "the three companies all blew their trumpets and smashed their jars, then grasped the torches in their left hands and the trumpets in their right, and shouted, 'A sword for Yahweh and for Gideon!' Every man stood where he was, all round the camp, and the whole camp leapt up in a panic and fled. The three hundred blew their trumpets, and throughout the camp Yahweh set every man against his neighbor" (Judge 7:20-22).

In the rout that followed, the three hundred completely devastated the Midianite horde.

Now there has been considerable desire to "explain" these stories and make them more historically plausible by suggesting (1) that it was an earthquake that leveled Jericho; (2) that Deborah figured that it was about time for the rains to come and had her forces located on Mt. Tabor with that in mind; and (3) that Gideon used the water test to locate his three hundred best men and then employed them in a very clever scheme. Certainly it is all right to get the stories historically "true," but we had better be careful that we do not *falsify* their meaning in the process. If the business is made to hinge entirely upon *natural* causes and *human* ingenuity, then we have simply another Nimrodian war and have canceled out everything the Bible wants to say about these being *God's* wars which he fought and won in his own way. But if you— with the biblical authors—can see earthquakes, rainstorms, etc., as being the deliberate activity *of God*, then explain away.

What we shall derive out of these three stories is a detailed pattern that constitutes the Old Testament doctrine of HOLY WAR. There is much more evidence for it than our three stories provide; but these will be sufficient for our purpose. Scholars cannot be specific as to just when and how the doctrine arose and where the idea came from. Our considerable use of the name "Joshua" intends him simply as a representative of the idea— without at all claiming him as its inventor and source. It is clear that the doctrine was at its height during the time of our stories, the general period described in the books of Joshua and Judges. We also can be quite certain when and why the doctrine went out of practice, during the time of David and following (that consideration we will save for a bit later). Even so, fragments of Holy War terminology can be spotted liberally scattered through the Psalms, the Prophets, and elsewhere. And as was suggested earlier, echoes of this sort of *thinking* permeate the Bible even through the New Testament.

Holy War is not an idea that is peripheral to the basic Old Testament *faith*. It is one of the central traditions *of* that faith; it belongs in the core right along with such traditions and practices as the Mosaic covenant, the kingship of Yahweh, the annual festivals, etc. Leave out this one, and you no longer have *the* Old Testament faith. Nor is this strand any less "religious" than those. Holy War *is* religion; and for these Hebrews, this sort of warring was every bit as much (and perhaps even more) a religious activity as were the prayers, sacrifices, rites, and festivals that we more customarily identify as "worship."

"Holy War" is the technical term used to identify the doctrine, although I do not believe that the exact phrase is to be found in Scripture itself. The wording actually is not strong enough to do justice to the case. Better is the phrase that is used a few times in the biblical text, "Yahweh's war." The most interesting occurrence is in Numbers 21:14, where there is cited and a quotation given from an ancient and now lost document entitled *The Book of the Wars of Yahweh*.

Although there is no way of proving it one way or another, there is the possibility that the author of Judges took his Song of Deborah from this earlier *Book of the Wars of Yahweh*. The quotation from that book which is found in the book of Numbers is *poetic*; and the Song of Deborah is a *poem* which certainly would be appropriate for a tome entitled *The Wars of Yahweh*. In any case, it is plain that "Yahweh's war" was a common enough idea in Israel that a whole volume of material could be gathered under the heading.

And to talk about "Yahweh's war" is not merely to say "a war fought *in the name of* God." We've had many of those in history—all too many; and they are *fake*. No, the Old Testament concept is that it is Yahweh who is *fighting* the war; about as much as is expected of the human participants is that they come along and watch him do it. Perhaps the clearest expression of the idea comes in a little incident from the Joshua-at-Jericho story:

> When Joshua came near Jericho he looked up and saw a man standing in front of him with a drawn sword in his hand. Joshua went up to him and said, "Are you for us or for our enemies?" And the man

said to him, "I am here as captain of the army of Yahweh." Joshua
fell down before him, face to the ground, and said, "What have you
to say to your servant, my lord?" The captain of Yahweh's army said
to him, "Take off your sandals; the place where you are standing is
holy"; and Joshua did so.

Joshua 5:13-15.

The commander of this army is not Joshua or any human being; the commander comes directly from God. And to obey that
command is "holy" activity; it is service to God himself.

Yet there have been so many wars fought in the name of
God; so many that have been claimed as being "God's war." In
fact, it would not be far wrong to suggest that for every war that
ever has been fought, there has been someone to claim that it is
God's work, that he is the sponsor of one side or the other. Yet, as
long as the sons of Adam are involved, one has to be suspicious
that it is *men* who are making the decisions and calling the shots
and then bringing in the *name of God* to give support to what
they have decided. In most instances there is strong evidence that
this is precisely what is going on. Is the case any different with the
Hebrew "wars of Yahweh"?

Well, all that can be said is that the Hebrew pattern has
some built-in safeguards against this happening. These people
were aware of the danger and worked to prevent it. And that is
very much to their credit. The evidence we will handle indicates a
very honest, careful, deliberate attempt to insure that it would
indeed be Yahweh's war and not a Nimrodian invention disguised
as such. And this we can say even though our final judgment is
that the Hebrews missed the thing they were trying for.

The first standard element in the Old Testament picture of
Holy War is "the draft," the call up, Selective Service, if you
please.

When Joshua and the children of Israel crossed the Jordan
and headed for Jericho, they were led by forty thousand fighting
men. "*Drafted for active service,* they crossed over to the lowlands

of Jericho in the presence of Yahweh to do battle" (Joshua 4:13; italics mine).

The Deborah story gets underway as she tells Barak: "These are the commands of Yahweh the God of Israel: 'Go and draw ten thousand men from Naphtali and Zebulun and bring them with you to Mount Tabor' " (Judges 4:6). Clearly, the intent is that this be *Yahweh's* call to arms, that the draft be at his initiative and under his sponsorship. Israel had no centralized government at this time; Deborah and Barak held no office and had no civil or religious authority of their own. Yahweh was doing the drafting.

Another detail comes through in the Gideon story: "Then the spirit of Yahweh took possession of Gideon; *he sounded the trumpet* and the Abiezrites were called out to follow him. He sent messengers all through Manasseh; and they too were called out. He sent messengers to Asher, Zebulun, and Naphtali, and they came up to meet the others" (Judges 6:34-35; italics mine). You recall that Gideon's draft was so successful that he got more than one hundred times the men he needed. And there is additional evidence elsewhere to indicate that the customary way of issuing Yahweh's call was by *trumpet*.

The Song of Deborah celebrates the quality of *response* that Yahweh's draft brings and raises a very modern issue:

> That the leaders took the lead in Israel,
>   that the people offered themselves willingly,
>   bless Yahweh! . . .
> My heart goes out to the commanders of Israel
>   who offered themselves willingly among the people.
>   Bless Yahweh. . . .
> Then down to the gates marched *the people of Yahweh* . . . .
>
> Then down marched the remnant of the noble;
>   *the people of Yahweh* marched down for him against
>   the mighty. . . .
> Among the clans of Reuben
>   there were great searchings of heart.
> Gilead stayed beyond the Jordan;

and Dan, why did he abide with the ships?
Asher sat still at the coast of the sea,
   settling down by his landings.
                    Judges 5:2, 9, 11, 13, 15-17, RSV; italics mine.

The main theme here, of course, is the *willingness* with
which the people offer themselves in Yahweh's service, even
though it means jeopardizing their very lives. Yet they trust him
implicitly and want nothing so much as to be "the people of
Yahweh." The phrase is a most significant one. Clearly, it signifies
a *westward* move back toward Eden rather than the eastward drift
that has marked our study thus far. "The people of Yahweh" is
the last title Adam, Cain, Nimrod, and company would welcome;
their whole intent was to be "their own men." We have a long
way to go yet before we will find peace; but here an all-important
corner has been turned: men willingly accepting Yahweh's draft
call and truly wanting to be his people, fighting his war in his way.

However, the last several lines of our text indicate that,
among some of the tribes, there was encountered what only can
be called *draft resistance*. And this leads to a consideration of the
comparable phenomenon today. In the biblical case, of course,
resistance to the draft of Yahweh is roundly condemned. However, if, precisely in order that he might answer *Yahweh's* call, a
person were to resist being drafted by a competing recruiter, that
would seem to make a lot of sense. After all, it was Jesus who said,
"No man can answer two draft calls" (or words to that effect). But
also, it would seem to be an entirely different thing for a person to
resist a call simply on the basis that he does not recognize the
claim of *any* authority upon him, that he will not answer to
anyone. Clearly, that attitude belongs to the old eastward drift
rather than our new westward movement.

Now how much of the draft resistance of our era has been
motivated by the desire to answer God's draft call and how much
by the desire to escape any and all drafts, period? Perhaps the
proper question to put to these resisters would be: "If you are
resisting the government's draft, whose would you *accept?*"

According to the Holy War pattern, simple acceptance of the draft call does not immediately qualify one for Yahweh's service. There is more involved in being one of "Yahweh's people." Joshua stated the matter as he addressed the people before the Jericho venture: *"Hallow yourselves,* for tomorrow Yahweh will do a great miracle among you" (Joshua 3:5; italics mine).

What does it mean to "hallow yourselves"? Basically it means "let Yahweh work you over, remodeling your Nimrodian image into that of himself until your total life and being become consistent with the war in which you have been enlisted to fight." We know at least some of the details that this hallowing involved for the ancient Hebrews.

It meant abstinence from sexual intercourse during one's term of service (1 Samuel 21:5 and 2 Samuel 11:11). For these Old Testament people, hallowing also involved the making of prayers and solemn vows to God, the offering of sacrifices, and the strict avoidance of those things that were considered ritually unclean. Of course, no one is inclined to maintain that the hallowing of *today's* "people of God" should follow the same formulas; but the fact that these ancients were willing to undergo rigorous discipline in becoming "formed" to the call they had accepted is an indicator of how truly serious they were in their desire that Yahweh's will and not their own be done, that Yahweh's war and not their own be fought.

Do our modern warriors—and particularly our "peace" warriors who at least aspire to be fighting God's war—show anything like the same intense desire to get every aspect of their lives consistent with their professed calling? You tell me. Is self-righteous disregard for other points of view consistent? Is hot, arrogant, abusive language consistent? Are violent or near-violent acts of obstruction or destruction consistent? Is plotting and chicanery consistent? Is the super-individualized escapism of drugs and liquor consistent? Are the depersonalizing effects of sexual promiscuity consistent? (But please don't tell me that what the establishment does is worse. I know that already, but I don't see what it has to do with whether God's people are serious about hallowing themselves into fit warriors.)

Now goodness knows, we find plenty of early Hebrew actions that strike us as being very inconsistent with what Yahweh's war actually is all about; and the remainder of the Bible will work at correcting those inconsistencies. Nevertheless, all the evidence suggests that these people were doing *the very best they knew how* in getting their lives hallowed in accordance with Yahweh's will. Their effort puts ours to shame.

Basic to the old Holy-War pattern is a standardized formula that occurs in the text time and time and time again. It appears in all three of our stories; in fact, in the Gideon account it occurs five times within the space of fifteen verses. With only slight variations according to the identity of the enemy, it reads: *Yahweh has given the enemy into your hands.*

There is a most interesting and significant detail involved here. The matter is stated as being accomplished fact. And yet it regularly comes at that point in the story at which the fact is very far from being accomplished, namely, even before the battle is joined. In effect, it becomes: "Go into the battle knowing that you already have won; Yahweh has done it for you." Such belief signifies complete faith in God, in his intention and power. It is a faith that goes far beyond "*we* shall overcome *someday*" to affirm that "*God* has overcome *already.*" Yet this is the quality of faith that the Bible teaches and demands throughout. Only such faith opens the possibility that true peace ever will come to our world.

And if that sort of promise is to come true, surely it can be only because Yahweh himself is there to do the fighting. His promise is not that the *army's* efforts will succeed but that he can guarantee the outcome because he knows that *his own* efforts do succeed. And this is precisely the way the matter comes across.

Joshua's orders to his troops are:

When you see the Ark of the Covenant of Yahweh your God being carried forward by the Levitical priests, then you too shall leave your positions and set out. Follow it, but do not go close to it; keep some distance behind, about a thousand yards. This will show you the way you are to go, for you have not travelled this way before.

Joshua 3:3-4.

The Ark represents the throne of Yahweh; and the significance of the order is that Yahweh is on hand to lead the engagement in person.

Then Deborah said to Barak, "Up! This day Yahweh gives Sisera into your hands. Already Yahweh has gone out to battle before you." So Barak came charging down from Mount Tabor with ten thousand men at his back. *Yahweh put Sisera to rout* with all his chariots and his army before Barak's onslaught.

Judges 4:14-15; italics mine.

Hurry up, boys, or Yahweh will have finished the job before we get there!

But it is the Gideon story that gives the most striking demonstration of this point. Gideon, recall, began with 32,000 men and cut the ranks to 300 before launching the attack. Many interpreters explain this as a weeding-out process in which Gideon was locating his very best men, the ones who would insure the success of his strategem. But if that were so, it would put the credit for the victory onto Gideon's cleverness, his ability as a commander, and the prowess of his hand-picked men. But the text itself explains the matter in an entirely contrary way:

Yahweh said to Gideon, "The people with you are more than I need to deliver Midian into their hands: Israel will claim the glory for themselves and say that it is their own strength that has given them the victory. Now make a proclamation for all the people to hear, that anyone who is scared or frightened to leave Mount Galud at once and go back home." . . . Yahweh said to Gideon, "With the three hundred men who lapped I will save you and deliver Midian into your hands, and all the rest may go home."

Judges 7:2-3, 7.

It wasn't that *Gideon* was trying to form the most effective fighting force; it was that *Yahweh* deliberately was forming a force ineffective enough to demonstrate that the victory was his doing and not theirs.

The meaning of this entire line of thought is best expressed in Joshua's farewell speech to his people:

> You must hold fast to Yahweh your God as you have done down to this day. For your sake Yahweh has driven out great and mighty nations; to this day not a man of them has withstood you. One of you can put to flight a thousand, because Yahweh your God fights for you, as he promised. Take very good care to love Yahweh your God.
>   Joshua 23:8-11.

And upon this point lies the heart of the matter for us, here and now, just as much as for them, then and there. If the war to establish the peaceable kingdom (the kingdom of God, which is the only truly peaceable kingdom) is fought on the basis of *our* numbers, our resources, our wisdom, our strategies, our good intentions, our peacemaking abilities, then it will fail; it is as simple as that. If, however, it is fought by God himself and by people who have put themselves totally under his command, then it does not make a great deal of difference what are our numbers, resources, etc.; there is no possible way the war *can* fail. The issue is not our *ability* but our *obedience*. Our success depends not upon the vision of what we can or will do but upon our faith that there is a God who already has given the victory into our hands *if we are but willing to accept it on his terms.* Joshua's statement of the matter cannot be improved: "Take very good care to love Yahweh your God."

The Holy War pattern picks up some of the implications that follow from the above. The word to Yahweh's people regularly is, "Fear not!"

When you take the field against an enemy and are faced by horses

and chariots and an army greater than yours, do not be afraid of
them; for Yahweh your God who brought you out of Egypt, will be
with you.

Deuteronomy 20:1.

"Have no fear," Moses answered; "stand firm and see the deliverance that Yahweh will bring you this day; for as sure as you see
the Egyptians now, you will never see them again. Yahweh will
fight for you; so hold your peace."

Exodus 14:13-14.

If one might venture an opinion, our contemporary peace
forces do not so much make a picture of those who are standing
firm, waiting to see the deliverance of Yahweh, as those who are
in frantic desperation, trying anything to gain a little ground.
Would that they might learn a little ancient Hebrew.

Panic does not belong with the people of Yahweh; it does
very much belong with the enemy. Rahab told the spies that the
heebie-jeebies had hit Jericho before Israel even had crossed the
river:

I know that Yahweh has given this land to you, that terror of you has
descended upon us all, and that because of you the whole country is
panic-stricken. For we have heard how Yahweh dried up the water
of the Red Sea before you when you came out of Egypt, and what
you did to Sihon and Og, the two Amorite kings beyond the Jordan,
whom you put to death. When we heard this, our courage failed us;
your coming has left no spirit in any of us; for Yahweh your God is
God in heaven above and earth below.

Joshua 2:9-11.

When the real thing got there, it took the form, of course, of
the blaring ram horns, a lot of wild shouting, and the clatter of
falling walls. In his farewell address, Joshua recalled and in-
terpreted the event by reporting some words of Yahweh:

The citizens of Jericho fought against you, but I delivered them into
your hands. I spread panic before you, and it was this, not your

sword or your bow, that drove out the two kings of the Amorites.
Joshua 24:11-12.

With Sisera and the Canaanites, it was the same thing all
over again: rain and mud, confusion and terror, people running
around like chickens with their heads cut off, and an impelling
desire to get out of there any way one could.

Gideon's is the best example of the screaming anxieties:

> The three companies all blew their trumpets and smashed their jars,
> then grasped their torches in their left hands and the trumpets in
> their right, and shouted, "A sword for Yahweh and for Gideon!"
> Every man stood where he was, all round the camp, and the whole
> camp leapt up in a panic and fled. The three hundred blew their
> trumpets, and throughout the camp Yahweh set every man against
> his neighbor.
>
> Judges 7:20-22.

That last sums things up and points us to our moral. There is
something self-defeating in the very nature of the Nimrodian
world; every man is pretty much against his neighbor even before
Yahweh gets in on it. Panic comes easy. Remember that all this
action takes place in the city called *Babel*. These people have only
as much security as they have been able to cobble together for
themselves; they have guilty consciences about having eaten ap-
ples and disobeyed God; and they have lost all their communication lines. When such is the state of affairs, even great big
enormous armies can disintegrate rather quickly when God puts a
little "boo" in them.

What this means for the Yahweh people (a point we shall
merely touch upon here and develop at length in a later chapter)
is that we don't need to feel it is incumbent upon us to go all out
in an obsessive attempt to track down Evil to his lair and do him
in at all costs. Time and the course of events are on our side; Evil
is not nearly as strong as he appears to be; and there is one who
stands ready to panic him into flight.

One of the most significant elements of the Holy War pat-

tern is also the one we find most repulsive. It is a practice known
as "the ban." We cannot determine historically just how often it
was used nor how the decision was made as to when it was to be
applied. But the clearest description of what it involved and what
it meant comes out of the story of Joshua at Jericho:

> "Yahweh has given you the city. The city shall be under solemn
> ban: *everything in it* belongs to Yahweh. No one is to be spared ex-
> cept the prostitute Rahab and everyone who is with her in the
> house, because she hid the men whom we sent. And you must
> beware of coveting anything that is forbidden under the ban; you
> must take none of it for yourselves; this would put the Israelite camp
> itself under the ban and bring trouble on it. All the silver and gold,
> all the vessels of copper and iron, shall be holy; they belong to
> Yahweh and they must go into Yahweh's treasury." ... Under the
> ban they destroyed everything in the city; they put everyone to the
> sword, men and women, young and old, and also cattle, sheep, and
> asses.... They then set fire to the city and everything in it, except
> that they deposited the silver and gold and the vessels of copper and
> iron in the treasury of Yahweh's house.
>
> Joshua 6:17-19, 21, 24; italics mine.

As we read material of this sort, the thing that inevitably im-
presses us is the cruelty, the bloodthirstiness, the depravity of the
action. It is right that we respond so; but if we are to be fair to
these people who were our forerunners in the faith, we ought to
swallow our feelings, read the account very carefully, and admit
that none of the motivation we see *in the event* actually is present
in the text. The stated motivation is something quite different
from depravity, is something that makes very good sense *from its
own perspective*, is something to which we ought to listen and
from which we ought to learn.

These people were very aware as to where lies the danger in
the doctrine of Holy War, in the whole procedure of claiming to
fight in Yahweh's war. It is the self-righteous justification of
Nimrodianism, of fighting for one's own selfish purposes and
using God's name to give a pious appearance to the affair. This is

the sin that besets man's war-making, his peacemaking, and everything else that he does. Indisputably, a great deal of our time and energy is spent in trying to make our selfish actions look godly. And of course, once this happens to Holy War, the whole idea becomes a blasphemous fraud.

How can that be protected against happening—as it has happened in most if not all of the so-called holy wars in history? The Hebrews devised a way; *the ban* was a vivid demonstration that the war was so completely Yahweh's doing and so completely for his purposes that the fighting men would neither claim nor keep any profit for themselves. It was the equivalent of putting one's whole paycheck into the offering plate. We ought to be willing to understand it so and give these people credit for what they were trying to do. The ban is the proof, the clearest possible witness to the fact that these Hebrews very deeply and sincerely wanted to be "the people of Yahweh," giving themselves totally to him, being restored to the image of God which is the ballerina posture. What evidence could we offer that *we* want that half as much or are willing to strive toward it with half the diligence that they did?

There may have been one final element in the Holy War pattern; the evidence does not allow us to say for sure. But it could be that the line, "To your tents, O Israel," was used as a signal that the war was over, that the victory was secure, that the rules of Holy War no longer were in effect, that everyone could go home.

What has this examination of Holy War shown us? We have seen that there is something eminently right and instructive about the doctrine as a whole and every point of it. Surely we have been helped. And yet ... and yet we *must* feel that there is here something badly wrong as well. It simply is impossible to reconcile the savage, city-leveling Yahweh of Joshua with the God and Father of Jesus. Where—even with their best intentions (better than ours)—did these old Hebrews get off the track? Let's retrace that track and see if we can find out.

They started with the assumption that Yahweh has a plan, something he has in mind to accomplish in this world, a kingdom he is intent to establish. In this they were right, very right. They realized, too, that there was in their midst that which was inclined to resist and oppose Yahweh's plan—and "that" meant WAR. In this, too, they were right, very right. They felt certain that Israel had been tabbed for a special role in Yahweh's plan. Right again. They were wise enough to see, however, that Israel was not herself the *end* of that plan, that Yahweh's purpose was not simply to heap favors upon Israel, that Israel was nothing or had done nothing to deserve such but rather had been chosen for use as an instrument in a larger plan. They were very right on this one, too, and deserve respect for seeing something that few peoples in this world (including ourselves) ever have accepted. The next one is a little more difficult to support from the texts, but it is quite possible that Joshua and company understood that the end of God's plan involved the totality of mankind, that his kingdom (the *peaceable* kingdom) was to be for all peoples without distinction. God's promise to Abraham, who lived long before Joshua, is recorded as: "By you all the families of the earth will bless themselves" (Genesis 12:3 RSV). And if they did understand it so, they were right on this one, too.

From this they should have drawn the conclusion that MAN IS NOT THE ENEMY. But this one they missed. It is not an easy truth to grasp—particularly so for finite man who must view God's plan from a rather limited, short-term, politically oriented perspective. As they saw it, God's plan includes an intention for Israel. Yet there are some people who threaten Israel's existence and would frustrate her God-given destiny. Therefore, if God's plan is to move forward, these people must be taken out of the way; it *must* be God's will and desire that we fight them.

The logic is altogether correct, but what also is involved is a failure of *faith* in the capabilities of God. *As far as man can see,* the only alternatives are either to let the plan of God be frustrated or to take out the obstructionists. And so he chooses what is obviously the least objectionable and most faithful alternative. But in actuality this is a Nimrodian decision based on the premise that *God's* alternatives are limited to what *man* can understand. "I can't figure out anything else that would work, so this *must* be what God wants me to do." But that is to desert obedience and God's help for action based on my own wisdom and resources.

Yet, on the other hand, if God's fight is *for the sake of man*, all men, then certainly he must have the wherewithal for getting us there without crunching some men, *any person*, in the process. This, then, is *faith*, true faith: to believe that God has ways of achieving his purpose without contradicting his purpose in the achieving of it—even when, from our position, we can't begin to imagine what those ways might be. That we get into binds where we can't act without contradicting ourselves is obvious; that God should get into such a bind is inconceivable.

But when the squeeze came, Israelite faith wasn't quite adequate, and the people fell back on the conclusion that man *must* be the enemy: there is no way for God's plan to go forward without fighting against men, so this must be what God wants. And once they were sure (or thought they were sure) of their conclusion, they followed God with a right good will—you have to give them credit for that!

But before we criticize ancient Israel for her failure of faith, we ought to ask ourselves whether we have done any better—we who have had Jesus and all sorts of advantages these earlier people did not have.

Clearly, anyone who sanctions war or violence under any circumstances has himself bought the premise that at least sometimes some men *must* be the enemy. He has no grounds for criticizing the Israelites. The most he can do is offer a political, Nimrodian judgment as to whether theirs was a *wise* war; and they have the same right to form a similar judgment about his. And nothing is so futile as an argument about which is a 'good' war.

But the question also must be asked whether many of our

peace advocates truly have accepted the proposition that man is *not* the enemy. They do show great concern about what happens to the poor and oppressed peoples of our world; but they give the impression that they couldn't care less what happens to presidents, government officials, and others who can be dismissed as "no-good militarists." They are much concerned when U.S. servicemen are killing people in pursuit of their goals. They are not all that concerned when third world revolutionaries and terrorists kill in pursuit of theirs. These people, too, then, have not really budged off the Israelite premise that the achievement of God's plan will require us to treat some men as enemy; and they have absolutely no ground for criticizing Joshua and company.

What it comes to is that, although many of us find the Joshua-Judges stories repulsive, there are few if any of us who have room to squawk.

We said earlier that the circumstances and causes of the demise of Holy War could be spotted with some certainty. Thereby hangs a tale. Israel's social and political evolution soon made Holy War completely outmoded and irrelevant. What happened is that the people decided that the attempt to operate under the direct leadership of Yahweh was impractical and that they needed a "government," some sort of institutionalized system that was a little more visible, predictable, and amenable to control. They set up a monarchy.

Through the brief reign of Saul and at least the early part of David's reign, the old tradition still carried enough weight that things did not change too much. But by the time we get to Solomon, the switchover is complete. Kings, of course, like to run their own wars in their own way ("After all, I *am* king here!"). And the first thing that has to be done is to get *organized*.

We will need trained and commissioned officers of different ranks who are on the job so that there always is someone available to get the war machine into instant action. We will need manuals, procedures, standardized maneuvers, etc., so that we will know what we're doing rather than just hatching some goofy scheme (such as Joshua's or Deborah's or Gideon's?) on the spur of the moment. Above all, we will need professional soldiers, skilled and equipped, ready on a standby basis for immediate use—and we will need a support system to back them up. In short, what we really need around here is a little "military *security.*" Oh, sure, we blundered through all right under the old system, but there was no *security;* we had nothing you could really count on, no way of knowing how things were going to turn out.

"But you have crowded Yahweh clear out of the picture!"

Not at all! *Not . . . at . . . all!* I am shocked that you have so completely misunderstood me. We are going to have *chaplains* who will pronounce God's blessing on our efforts and continually remind us that we are fighting for the glory of Yahweh! No; bypassing Yahweh is the furthest thing from our minds; all we are after is a little *security.*

And thus did Israel get with it and join *us* in our modern, institutionalized, secularized, de-faithed concept of war. The move, very clearly, is away from any concept of ballerinas joining Yahweh in *his* war; it is, rather, a great jump to the east, where Nimrod now is going to build some security for himself in his own way and out of his own resources.

The loss of Holy War was a great retrogression for mankind and a situation which, if anything, has continued to deteriorate right down to our own day. From Holy War it would be a comparatively short step to get corrected the understanding of who is the enemy and how he is to be fought. But there is no way . . . no way to get from Nimrodian war to the peaceable kingdom of God.

We never have said that Joshua had all the answers, that he is the equal of Jesus; such simply is not the case. Nevertheless, modern man—even most modern *Christians*—are in no position to dismiss, criticize, or put down Joshua. Until we try as hard to be "the people of Yahweh" as he and his compatriots did, he had better be looked up to and emulated. Holy War is the only starting point from which to get to Holy Peace.

3
It's His War.
Let Him Fight It!

See how the oppressor has met his end and his frenzy ceased!
Yahweh has broken the rod of the wicked,
   the scepter of the ruler
   who struck down peoples in his rage with unerring blows,
   who crushed nations in anger
   and persecuted them unceasingly.
The whole world has rest and is at peace;
   it breaks into cries of joy.

—Isaiah 14:4-7

Our title for this chapter may be a little crude to do justice to Isaiah's thought, but it does express the general drift of where we are headed.

Our subject is the prophet Isaiah; Gerhard von Rad is still providing the cues. Nevertheless, we will not attempt to cut things as fine as von Rad does. He attempts to correlate particular passages with particular times and events in the prophet's career and to separate Isaiah's work from later material that may have become included with his. We will be content simply to find the basic pattern of thought underlying the book as a whole. There is no doubt but that it represents the prophet's own understanding.

Isaiah comes approximately five hundred years after Joshua and probably two hundred fifty years after all practice of Holy War had ceased. He lived in a highly organized nation-state named Judah, centered around its grand and sophisticated capital of Jerusalem, ruled by hereditary monarchs, the descendants of King David. War was a thoroughly secular and professional operation—and one with which Isaiah was well familiar. All during the prophet's career, Judah was caught up in the power struggle between the two military behemoths, Assyria to the north and east and Egypt to the south and west. The nation experienced frequent encroachments and lived under the threat of imminent extinction—a thoroughly modern situation.

Although a quarter of a millennium has passed since Holy War last was practiced, it will be evident that Isaiah is familiar with this way of thinking and accepts its basic validity. At the same time, he chooses also to use some other traditions and some insights of his own to supplement and modify the inherited pattern.

> Yahweh of Hosts has sworn:
> In very truth, as I planned, so shall it be;
>> as I designed, so shall it fall out:
>>> I will break the Assyrian in my own land. . . .
> This is the plan prepared for the whole earth,
> this the hand stretched out over all the nations.
>> For Yahweh of Hosts has prepared his plan:
>>> who shall frustrate it?
> His is the hand stretched out, and who shall turn it back?
>
> Isaiah 14:24-27.

Isaiah agrees with Joshua that Yahweh has something in mind, a purpose and a plan, and that, because resistance has shown itself, this means war. Isaiah would have been as willing as Joshua to identify this conflict as "the war (or wars) of Yahweh." And he would have been just as confident as Joshua that, Yahweh being who he is, it is utterly inconceivable that his intentions might finally be frustrated.

However, Isaiah's understanding of that plan is much more clear and detailed than what Joshua and company had achieved. There we encountered considerable vagueness as to what final end Yahweh had in mind, who all it would involve, and how it would work out. About as far as the earlier understanding went was that Yahweh wills the establishment and perpetuation of Israel. Whoever, then, is pro-Israel is on Yahweh's side, a "good guy"; whoever is opposed to Israel is a "bad guy" to be wiped out.

Now, with Isaiah, the matter becomes much more subtle and complex—and undoubtedly much nearer the truth. As our text makes clear, Yahweh's is a plan for the whole earth. And as subsequent quotations will disclose, it is a plan for the *peace and well-being* of the whole earth. Yet, even though the plan is *universal* in its scope and intent, it also is specific enough that Isaiah can say what is to happen to Assyria (in this instance). From one standpoint, the plan still would have to be called "pro-Israel" but not in nearly as simplistic a sense as had been done earlier; the old pattern of "us good guys" versus "you bad guys" gets broken up completely. Much is taken over from Holy War thinking, but much is changed as well.

For Isaiah, the key to Yahweh's plan is his promise for ZION. No matter what happens anywhere else, no matter if everything else goes, Zion will be preserved. If needs be, Yahweh will intervene dramatically at the very last moment; but Zion shall never fall. Its existence is the very hinge of God's plan for the world.

> Look, I am laying a stone in Zion, a block of granite,
> a precious corner-stone for a firm foundation;
> he who has faith shall not waver.
>
> Isaiah 28:16.

In another connection, although with the Zion tradition probably still in mind, Isaiah says: "Have firm faith, or you will not stand firm" (7:9). For him, *faith* almost amounts to a confidence that, whatever might happen, Yahweh will bring his Zion plan to pass.

It seems certain that the roots of the Zion tradition go back some time before Isaiah; it also finds expression, for instance, in many of the Psalms and elsewhere. When it originated or how, we cannot tell; but there is no doubt that Isaiah is the one who picked it up, enlarged and developed it, and gave it its most outstanding demonstration. That the Zion tradition is itself a special category of Holy War will become obvious.

"Zion," originally, designated the particular hilltop which was the location of Jerusalem, when the city was still very small. The location was made to order for military defense, and the city itself was a walled fortress, so the term "Zion" carried connotations of "an impregnable stronghold." Later, after the city had expanded far beyond the one hilltop and after the temple had been built, even though the temple stood on a different peak, the terminology shifted to make "Zion" a reference to the temple area. This is the situation in Isaiah's writings.

Yet the sheer existence of the temple does not get to the heart of his concern either. If, for instance, the temple were to remain standing but all the people be destroyed, it is doubtful that Isaiah would consider that a true preservation of Zion. On the other hand, it is plain that Zion is not a symbolic representation either of the whole of Israel's (Judah's) territory or the whole of her people; the prophet sees that both of these can and will be decimated. Rather, Zion seems to stand for *true loyalty to Yahweh*, even when reduced to a bare minimum of space (one hilltop) and a bare minimum of people. The amount of such loyalty may undergo drastic reduction, but God will step in directly before he will let it disappear altogether. Indeed, Isaiah's concept of "Zion" would seem to be very closely related to his more familiar theme regarding the "remnant" that will be preserved.

This idea (although not always couched in Zion terminology) will be constant throughout the remainder of our study and a very important element in it. The Zion tradition asserts that the cause of God's peace cannot suffer final defeat and that the coming of that peace is guaranteed by God himself. Further, that coming is not dependent upon the gradual and continuous growth either of some sort of "peace movement" or even of Yahweh worship (the church) itself. God has the capability of bringing peace even out of the situation that seems most hopeless and destitute of peace.

But that the destiny of Zion lies in its coming to be the center of universal peace, Isaiah makes very clear:

> In days to come
> the mountain of Yahweh's house [Zion, of course]
> shall be set over all other mountains,
> lifted high above the hills.
> All the nations shall come streaming to it
> and many peoples shall come and say,
> "Come, let us climb up on to the mountain of Yahweh,
> to the house of the God of Jacob,
> that he may teach us his ways
> and we may walk in his paths."
> For instruction issues from Zion,
> and out of Jerusalem comes the word of Yahweh;
> he will judge between nations,
> arbiter among many peoples.
> They shall beat their swords into mattocks
> and their spears into pruning-knives;
> nation shall not lift sword against nation
> nor ever again be trained for war.
> O people of Jacob, come,
> let us walk in the light of Yahweh.
>
> Isaiah 2:2-5.

Another very important idea is related to the picture of Zion-centered peace when the prophet speaks of a coming king who (presumably from Zion) will establish the new era:

> All the boots of trampling soldiers
> and the garments fouled with blood

shall become a burning mass, fuel for the fire.
For a boy has been born for us, a son given to us
    to bear the symbol of dominion on his shoulder;
    and he shall be called
    in purpose wonderful, in battle God-like,
    Father for all time, Prince of Peace.

Great shall the dominion be,
    and boundless the peace
bestowed on David's throne and on his kingdom,
to establish it and sustain it
    with justice and righteousness
    from now and for evermore.
The zeal of Yahweh of Hosts shall do this.

                                        Isaiah 9:5-7.

No Christian can read these lines without being pointed to
the commander he serves. Faith in the preservation of Zion and
the accomplishment of its peace is destined to become faith in the
Prince of Peace who will establish and sustain that peace with justice and righteousness.

The end and purpose of Zion is that, through the services of
the coming Prince of Peace, it become the source and center for
that state of worldwide peace which the New Testament calls
"the kingdom of God." But how are the events of Zion to get us
from here to there? Isaiah speaks to this matter.

One of his basic assumptions stands in rather strong contrast
to what we found earlier in Holy War thinking:

I have sons whom I reared and brought up,
but they have rebelled against me.
The ox knows its owner
    and the ass its master's stall;
but Israel, my own people,
has no knowledge, no discernment. . . .
[You] have deserted Yahweh,
spurned the Holy One of Israel
and turned your backs on him. . . .

> Your head is covered with sores,
>   your body diseased;
> from head to foot there is not a sound spot in you—
> nothing but bruises and weals and raw wounds. . . .
> Your country is desolate, your cities lie in ashes.
> Strangers devour your land before your eyes;
> it is desolate as Sodom in its overthrow.
>   Only Zion is left.
>   Isaiah 1:2-8.

Notice, first of all, that Isaiah defines sin in precisely the same terms Genesis did: it is the desire to desert the ballerina role, spurn God, and turn one's back on him. However, even though the old Holy War concept reckoned at least with the *possibility* that Israel herself might be sinful (the need to be hallowed, the ban's protection against self-interest, etc.), nevertheless, the rather easy assumption was made that the Israelites were pure enough in intent and motive that they could fight with Yahweh in *his* war, could claim that their fighting was, in fact, *his* war.

But if the case is as Isaiah suggests, that Israel, the one people of the world that stands closest to Yahweh, is herself in complete rebellion against any ballerina role, then there arises a question which, in due course, Isaiah will bring us to face directly: "Is there now, or has there ever been, a people righteous and well-intentioned enough that they can claim that their fighting is, in fact, the war of Yahweh? Is there any group good enough to be Yahweh's army?"

In the final verse of our text, the prophet undoubtedly has in mind the actual military devastation of Judah and Jerusalem. But surely he must have had even more prominently in mind the *spiritual* devastation which was a fact even before the military devastation took place. Only Zion (a bare remnant of true worship and loyalty) was left even before only Zion (a little Jerusalem hilltop) was left. His evaluation of Israel's relationship to Yahweh is very different from that which characterized the old Holy War thinkers.

> Shame on you! who make unjust laws
> and publish burdensome decrees,
> depriving the poor of justice,
> robbing the weakest of my people of their rights,
> despoiling the widow and plundering the orphan.
> What will you do when called to account,
> when ruin from afar confronts you?
>
>   Isaiah 10:1-3.

Now, far from being the ones who are carrying Yahweh's war to the "bad guys," the Israelites turn out to be those who, through their own wickedness, are bringing war upon themselves. And if this is so with Israel, with how many other nations in history must it be the case that, although they like to see themselves as defenders of the truth, their wars actually are nothing more than the fruit of their own falsity?

Our text reveals, too, that the desire to go it alone and be *like God* inevitably perverts one's man-to-man relationships at the same time. Rebellion against God and misuse of the other person ultimately come to the same thing.

> Shame upon those who go down to Egypt for help
>   and rely on horses,
> putting their trust in chariots many in number
> and in horsemen in their thousands,
> but do not look to the Holy One of Israel
>   or seek guidance of Yahweh! . . .
> The Egyptians are men, not God,
> their horses are flesh, not spirit;
> and, when Yahweh stretches out his hand,
> the helper will stumble and he who is helped will fall,
>   and they will all vanish together.
>
>   Isaiah 31:1-3.

Here Isaiah explicitly brands Israel's military preparedness—her arms and alliances and whatever—as being part of her *sin,* as a particular sign of her failure to trust in Yahweh and his promise for Zion and mankind. And this preparedness, it should be pointed out, was totally *defensive* in character. Isaiah is not condemning only aggressive, imperialistic warfare—such was completely beyond possibility or dream for Israel at this point. No, Israel's very desire to take over her own defense, to create security for herself, is an aspect of her Nimrodian defiance of God.

> Oh, rebel sons! says Yahweh,
> you make plans, but not of my devising,
> you weave schemes, but not inspired by me,
> piling sin upon sin;
> you hurry down to Egypt without consulting me,
> to seek protection under Pharaoh's shelter
> and take refuge under Egypt's wing.
>
> Isaiah 30:1-2.

Israel, we are told, had a plan—and that a "peace plan," it should be said. Instead of arming for her own defense, she would count upon the Egyptian military to provide that. As peace plans go, this one is not at all bad; it keeps Israel out of the arms race, involves her in disarmament (or unarmament), and is entirely nonaggressive. Yet Yahweh condemns it, not because it is a *poor* plan, but because it is not *his* plan. And by that way of thinking, how many of our modern and even *Christian* peace plans do you think would evoke God's criticism?

It is important to be reminded that the entire analysis above is directed to *Israel,* the people which, according to the understanding both of the prophet and his hearers, had been especially chosen by Yahweh and had received all sorts of advantages and guidance from him. If, even at this, Israel was so far out of line that she could not possibly fight Yahweh's war, then certainly the same would be true for any other people that might be considered.

So Isaiah is saying, in effect, that there is no such thing as a *just war,* because there are no peoples who themselves are just enough to fight them. The motives of even the best of peoples are impure and sinful enough that any wars they fight are bound to be sinful, too.

This thought calls for investigation. Most of the wars fought in history—and particularly those of the nations of Judeo-Christian background—have been defended on the grounds that they were "just wars." That is to say, they were wars properly fought for noble and righteous ends, the accomplishment of peace, justice, and the enhancement of humane living—that, in effect, they were part of Yahweh's war and were blessed by him.

Yet Isaiah's observations about Israel force us to take a closer look. Even if we concentrate upon those wars which were most strongly claimed as being of God, serious doubts begin to obtrude themselves. If, on the one hand, God is identified as the Father of Jesus Christ and his character defined by what we have seen in Jesus; and if, on the other, we look closely at the way in which these wars were fought, the spirit that pervaded their fighting, and the consequences that followed; it seems less and less likely that they should be justified as being of God. More and more they take on the smell of being "plans, but not of my devising, . . . schemes, but not inspired by me."

For instance, we have examined the stated rationale that stood behind the Holy War practice of the ban. There is no reason to doubt the practitioners' sincerity and honest desire to obey Yahweh. Nevertheless, when one (and particularly a Christian) contemplates the hideous carnage that the ban required and encouraged, when he considers the completely indiscriminate and merciless slaughter of innocent men, women, and children, he cannot help but feel that the event reflects more of human presumption than it does of divine obedience. In the same way, although the Crusaders sincerely thought themselves to be fighting for the cause of Christ, the Crusades show much more of the character of the sinful-human than they do of the righteous-divine. Even the best of people with the best of intentions are not sufficiently godlike that they can fight God's war without corrupting and perverting it with their own Nimrodian tendencies.

And if Isaiah's analysis hits the pro-war fighters of "just wars," it also hits the fighters of the *anti*-war "just war." Anti-war

movements often tend to display many of the markings of another
"just war" or "holy crusade." One is led to wonder whether these
are not again "plans not of my devising, schemes not inspired by
me." I have in mind such things as an arrogant sense of one's own
righteousness that invites one to pass easy judgments on whoever
happens not to agree; a lack of any self-doubt or suspicion, showing itself in a quick readiness to instruct others about what they
ought to do; a lust for power and a desire to control; and a willingness, for the sake of one's "just cause," to flirt with violence
(verbal violence against persons; violence against honesty, fair
play, and aboveboardness; violence against property and the
rights of others).

Just because the pro-war position is wrong, it does not follow
that each and every anti-war position is right. In his day, Isaiah
felt free to question the motives of his own people, the Israelite
"good guys." I am confident that he would be just as free in
examining the motives of the good-guy party today. Knowing
what is in man, we need to be suspicious of any group that claims
the righteousness of being God's warriors; we need to be suspicious even of ourselves—*especially* of ourselves.

> Be warned: the Lord, Yahweh of Hosts,
> is stripping Jerusalem and Judah
>   of every prop and stay. . . .
> Your men shall fall by the sword,
>   and your warriors in battle;
> then Zion's gates shall mourn and lament,
> and she shall sit on the ground stripped bare.
>   Isaiah 3:1, 25-26.

And now hear this one, if you can! Because of Israel's sin, the
war of Yahweh is directed *against* Zion—against the very Zion he
has promised to preserve as the world peace center. "That is a
strange one!" It is, and Isaiah knows it.

> But Yahweh shall arise as he rose on Mount Perazim
> and storm with rage as he did in the Vale of Gibeon

> to do what he must do—how strange a deed!
> to perform his work—how outlandish a work!
>   But now have done with your arrogance,
>   lest your bonds grow tighter;
>   for I have heard destruction decreed
> by the Lord Yahweh of Hosts for the whole land.
>   Isaiah 28:21-22.

It is an outlandish business; but Yahweh is doing "what he *must* do"—Israel has forced him to it. However, this is not to say that he has switched sides, faulted on his promise, or changed goals. His work may be strange, but that does not mean that it is without rhyme or reason.

> Once again I will act against you
> to refine away your base metal as with potash
>   and purge all your impurities;
> I will again make your judges what once they were
>   and your counsellors like those of old.
> Then at length you shall be called
> the home of righteousness, the faithful city.
>   Justice shall redeem Zion
>   and righteousness her repentant people.
>   Isaiah 1:25-27.

Yahweh's apparent action *against* Israel, seen in its true perspective, is discovered to be a necessary action *for* Israel. It is intended for the *redemption* of Zion. Although it is indeed a strange work, it is a greater and more loving deed for Yahweh to fight *against* Zion for her refining than to fight *with* her against her enemies. We now have come an entire level deeper into the mind and purpose of God than the old doctrine of Holy War ever could take us. Would that we might be open and ready to be helped when God must fight against *us*—as we most certainly force him to do!

> I have given my warriors their orders
> and summoned my fighting men to launch my anger;
>   they are eager for my triumph.

> Hark, a tumult in the mountains, the sound of a vast
>   multitude;
> hark, the roar of kingdoms, of nations gathering!
> Yahweh of Hosts is mustering a host of war,
> men from a far country, from beyond the horizon.
>   It is Yahweh with the weapons of his wrath
>   coming to lay the whole land waste.
>   Isaiah 13:3-5.

Here the reversal is complete. This clearly is old Holy War language about Yahweh mustering an army and leading it to battle. But the application is the direct opposite of what we saw earlier: Yahweh's army is composed of foreigners, the enemies of Israel, and he will fight through them to decimate Israel herself.

We need to be careful about the implications at this point. Is this to say that the nations have replaced Israel in God's plan? have now taken on the ballerina role? have achieved a righteousness superior to Israel's? are good enough to fight Yahweh's war with him? have become his obedient and useful servants?

No! The nations may form Yahweh's army, but the rest does not follow. Isaiah is very clear on this point:

> The Assyrian! He is the rod that I wield in my anger,
> and the staff of my wrath is in his hand.
> I send him against a godless nation,
> I bid him march against a people who rouse my wrath,
> to spoil and plunder at will
> and trample them down like mud in the streets.
> But this man's [i.e., the Assyrian's] purpose is lawless,
> lawless are the plans in his mind;
>   for his thought is only to destroy
> and to wipe out nation after nation. . . .
>   When Yahweh has finished all that he means to do
> on Mount Zion and in Jerusalem, he will punish the
> king of Assyria for this fruit of his pride and for
> his arrogance and vainglory, because he said:
>   By my own might I have acted
> and in my own wisdom I have laid my schemes.
>   Isaiah 10:5-7, 12-13.

In another passage, Isaiah describes the sin of Assyria in words that might have been written to order for recalling our themes from Genesis: becoming *like God*, Nimrod, and the tower of Babel:

> How you have fallen from heaven, bright morning star,
> felled to the earth, sprawling helpless across the nations!
>   You thought in your own mind,
>   I will scale the heavens;
> I will set my throne high above the stars of God,
>   I will sit on the mountain where the gods meet
>   in the far recesses of the north.
>   I will rise high above the cloud-banks
>   and make myself *like the Most High*.
>
> Isaiah 14:12-14; italics mine.

Notice that the prophet presents Yahweh as scoring *Assyria* for precisely the same sin that he earlier had scored *Israel*. Israel's military alliances and Assyria's making of war *both* are condemned as schemes hatched in disregard and defiance of God. We tend to think that, if one party in a dispute is wrong, the other must be right. Particularly, those who (perhaps in all propriety) focus upon the wrongs of the U.S. government often wind up justifying all sorts of wrongs on the part of other nations. But Isaiah finds no distinction of comparative righteousness between Israel and Assyria; indeed, his language against Yahweh's army (the Assyrians) is perhaps even harsher than that against Yahweh's enemy (Israel).

The thought is subtle at this point, but let us attempt to untangle it. It could be put in a most maddening way: "Was Assyria doing God's will in attacking and devastating Israel?" Yes, we are told as much. "Yet Yahweh was determined to punish Assyria?" Right. "Why?" For *not* doing Yahweh's will ... *while she was doing Yahweh's will!*

There would seem to be but one way of making sense of all this. It was *not* God's will that Assyria be a destroyer intent to "wipe out nation after nation"; that was Assyria's own choice, done in arrogance and vainglory as a scheme laid in her own apple-type wisdom. However, once that choice had been made and was a matter of fact, Yahweh could *use* it as a means of forwarding his own holy purpose for Zion. In this sense, then, Assyria *was* doing Yahweh's will and properly could be identified as the army of Yahweh. Because God grants people and nations freedom, they can do that which he does not *approve;* but because he has some freedom of his own, he can *use* even that which he does not *approve* in the achievement of his own purposes. Yet, the fact that God can use something for good reflects no credit or approval on the *agent*, who intended it quite otherwise.

This principle is a very important one, and one that we will find helpful at any number of points. It is closely related to what we found back in Genesis, when Yahweh made tunics of skins for the man and woman. Yahweh did not *approve* of man's wearing clothes; it was only human sinfulness that made them necessary. But once man *did* need them, God was willing to provide them and *use* them as a means toward getting man back to what he should be. Does clothing, then, represent God's will for man? Yes and no; there isn't any other correct way to answer.

The principle also can help ease our frustration as regards Holy War. Was it God's will, did he *want* Israel to level cities and slaughter entire populations under the ban? It is very difficult to see how he could *approve* such action; this *must* represent a misunderstanding on Israel's part—perhaps a sincere *effort* to find God's will but, even so, a decision still too much colored by man's tendency to be *like God* and depend upon one's own wisdom.

In discussing this problem of Holy War, John Howard Yoder has pointed out that a parent, speaking to a four-year-old child, might well insist that he have nothing to do with matches and yet tell the same child, at fourteen, to go get some matches and start a fire. Obviously, in that situation it is neither the character and wisdom of the parent nor the significance and potential of matches that has changed; what *has* changed is the understanding and competency of the child. This thought is helpful but does not really satisfy the question as to whether God specifically told the ancient Hebrews mercilessly to slaughter their enemies. So let's try it from a slightly different angle.

Even when Scripture says, "Thus says the Lord," what then stands recorded is obviously a report of what human beings *heard* him say rather than the unmediated *voice* of God himself. In by far the greater number of cases this presents no problem at all; the words reported are entirely consistent with what all our knowledge of God would lead us to expect. But when the words run entirely contrary to what all that knowledge would lead us to expect, we should perhaps question the *hearing* of the reporters rather than the consistency of God's *speaking*. It is true that God is likely to have said something different to his four-year-old children from what he did to his fourteen-year-olds. Yet it is also true that what four-year-olds (ancient Hebrews standing at the beginning of God's self-revelation) report as having *heard* about matches is not likely to be as accurate as what is reported by fourteen-year-olds (Christians who have had the privilege not only of *more* of God's self-revelation but also its *consummation* in the person of the Lord Jesus)—although, of course, the problem of four-year-olds is with their *understanding* and not their ears.

Does this mean, then, that Israel was mistaken and that God was *not* present and active in the wars of the Conquest? No, it does not mean that; rather, once Israel had determined that she was going to fight, God determined that, whether he *approved* of such fighting or not, he was going to *use* it to preserve Israel, give her a homeland, and lead her in the way toward the peaceable kingdom. Nevertheless, it dare never be concluded that God's righteous *use* of the situation thereby makes Israel's original decision *right*. So, did Israel's holy wars represent the will of God? Yes and no; there isn't any other correct way to answer.

Was it God's will that Jesus die on the cross? Obviously the men who hung him there were doing an evil thing and something that God in no way could *approve*. But once it was done, God could and did *use* it as the best thing that ever happened, a source

of infinite good. However, this in no way excuses the evil of having crucified him. Was it God's will that he be executed on the
cross? Yes and no; there isn't any other correct way to answer.

What Isaiah tells us here about the warring of Israel and
Assyria probably also should be taken as applying to all other
wars, past, present, and future. The prophet does not portray God
as *approving* any war makers, no matter who they are or for what
they are fighting. But this is not to say that war simply is *outside*
of God's plan, purpose, and control, that it has no significance or
utility in his eyes. Quite the contrary, war is the punishment
brought upon themselves by those who foster and create the kind
of situations that lead to war. And it is not that the losing nation is
the punished one and the winner merely the punisher. War always is punishment both ways. For example, Jacques Ellul points
out how widely totalitarian ideology and practice have infected
the camp of the Allies since we fought—and supposedly defeated—the totalitarian Nazis. Our way of fighting contaminated
us with the very thing we were fighting against; and this is the
punishment that is built into the very nature of human warfare. It
safely can be said that no nation ever has gone to war without
hurting itself in the process.

We are not meaning to say that no innocent *persons* ever get
hurt in war. We are saying that there are no innocent parties to
war, no innocent, righteous nations or armies involved in wars.
War is the punishment that nations, through their sinfulness,
bring upon themselves. And thus the presence of war in our midst
is evidence not that God's world is operating wrong but that it is
operating right, as it should. It is right that bad actions have bad
consequences—otherwise there would be absolutely no hope of
betterment for the world. And God's efforts in history are directed
not toward protecting men from the consequences of their actions
(although, as we have seen, he does cushion them from having to
take the full shock) but in getting their actions changed so that the
consequences can and automatically will be different.

Thus war is not some sort of accidental aberration that we

ought to be able to manipulate out of the system of history. War is
the just and proper consequence of, the appropriate symptom and
pain for, the misbehavior that causes it. And fortunately, as God
would have it, the pain will not finally quit or the symptoms go
away merely through the aspirin-like ministrations of treaties,
pacts, alliances, and all such political arrangements. These are to
be welcomed for the relief they bring, but there can be no satisfy-
ing cure short of the nations themselves being radically transformed and healed by getting right with God.

Is war right in God's eyes? Yes and no; there isn't any other
correct way to answer.

Back to Isaiah, with Zion itself being threatened and the rest
of the country actually occupied by the Assyrian "army of
Yahweh," we come to the heart of the ancient Zion tradition.

> Listen! it is the thunder of many people,
> they thunder with the thunder of the sea.
> Listen! it is the roar of nations
> roaring with the roar of mighty waters.
> When he rebukes them, away they fly,
> driven like chaff on the hills before the wind,
>   like thistledown before the storm.
> At evening all is confusion,
>   and before morning they are gone.
> Such is the fate of our plunderers,
>   the lot of those who despoil us.
>   Isaiah 17:12-14.

> Then suddenly, all in an instant, . . .
> all her oppressors themselves
> shall fade as a dream, a vision of the night.
>   Isaiah 29:5, 7.

> So shall Yahweh of Hosts come down to battle
>   for Mount Zion and her high summit.
> Thus Yahweh of Hosts, like a bird hovering over its
>   young,

will be a shield over Jerusalem;
   he will shield her and deliver her,
   standing over her and delivering her. . . .
Assyria shall fall by the sword, but by no sword of man;
   a sword that no man wields shall devour him.
                              Isaiah 31:4-5, 8.

Here is the turning point in God's work and in Israel's fortunes—and notice that it is entirely Yahweh's doing, without assistance from anyone. If one chose to do so, he could put it that Yahweh now fights *against* Yahweh's army (which is how Assyria and the nations were identified earlier). But I hope no one does choose to put it so; it only would reconfuse the situation that we did have pretty well clarified.

In any case, Isaiah told us earlier that Yahweh's army attacking Zion was God's *strange* and *outlandish* work. But now, the action which truly turns things around and puts Zion on the way toward actually becoming the peace center of the world . . . this action is God's *proper* work. And note well: this proper work is *not* a case of *Israel* fighting against Assyria; on this point Isaiah has moved entirely beyond the old Holy War pattern. God's proper work, the work that carries his *approval* as well as his *use*, must be achieved by a sword *not of man*. Human swords (actually, the humans who wield the swords) inevitably are corrupted by too much of apple-knowledge and Nimrodianism to be effective in Yahweh's proper work of creating justice and peace.

Although Israel's asking for punishment and Assyria's all-too-willing eagerness to dish it out put Yahweh in position where he could *use* the human sword, nowhere in Isaiah is there expressed any *approval* of its use. And when it comes to God's proper work of creating peace, justice, and righteousness, the human sword explicitly is disallowed. Consider, too, that, if God was capable of preserving Zion without human help at that time, he is capable of preserving whatever ought to be preserved today. There is no reason to believe that any situation ever has arisen or ever could arise that would move Isaiah to change his counsel.

But please don't ask what is this "sword that no man wields"
or how it operates; that is, don't ask *how* God wins his victory over
human rebellion and brings Zion to be the tallest of the mountains, the mountain of peace. Isaiah doesn't tell us—which is why
our book will need some more chapters.

At several points in his work Isaiah gives us a capsule description of the entire course of events that we have traced thus far.
They will serve to pull our thoughts together and display some
facets that call for particular attention.

> Today he [i.e., the enemy] is due to pitch his camp in
>   Nob;
>   he gives the signal to advance
>   against the mount of the daughter of Zion,
>   the hill of Jerusalem.
>   Look, the Lord, Yahweh of Hosts,
>   cleaves the trees with a flash of lightning,
> the tallest are hewn down, the lofty laid low,
>   the heart of the forest is felled with the axe
>   and Lebanon with its noble trees has fallen.
>   Then a shoot shall grow from the stock of Jesse,
>   and a branch shall spring from his roots. . . .
> Round his waist he shall wear the belt of justice,
>   and good faith shall be the girdle round his body.
>   Then the wolf shall live with the sheep,
>   and the leopard lie down with the kid. . . .
> They shall not hurt or destroy in all my holy mountain;
>   for as the waters fill the sea,
> so shall the land be filled with the knowledge of Yahweh.
>   Isaiah 10:32—11:1, 5-6, 9.

The punishing invader makes his way across Israel, wreaking
havoc as he comes. He camps at Nob, just outside of Jerusalem,
and then launches his assault directly against Zion. At this point
Yahweh comes crashing in like a thunderbolt leveling a forest. Apparently Isaiah has it in mind that the trees representing both the
invader and Israel are broken off; because in the following (after
how long a time lapse we are not told), one of the stumps sends

forth a new shoot. That the stump is "the stock of Jesse" tells us
that the shoot is a descendant of King David. Leaving at that
point his forest analogy, Isaiah makes it plain that this coming
king is the same one whom he elsewhere identified as the Prince
of Peace. Through his reign of justice and truth, Yahweh is made
known and peace comes to the entire earth.

> Howl in the gate, cry for help in the city,
>   let all Philistia be in turmoil;
>   for a great enemy is coming from the north,
>   not a man straying from his ranks.
> What answer is there for the envoys of the nation?
> This, that Yahweh has fixed Zion in her place,
> and the afflicted among his people shall take refuge there.
>   Isaiah 14:31-32.

Here is an amazing little oracle, for it is directed not to Israel
but to Philistia. Over the centuries, the Philistines had been the
worst among Israel's traditional enemies; there was very bad
blood between them. At the time of the oracle, Philistia is
threatened with extinction; the expected response would be for Israel to say, "Good riddance!" What hope, then, is there—if any—
for the Philistines? Isaiah says that their one hope lies in what
Yahweh (who is not their God) is doing in Zion (which is not their
territory and which is, indeed, a place they would have been
happy to demolish). *God's action in Zion is intended as much for
the salvation of the Philistines as for the Israelites.* We may not
find it surprising that Yahweh should act so; we ought to be sur-
prised to find an Israelite prophet teaching it and Israelite tradition preserving that teaching.

The line of thought gets even more spectacular in the following. The enemy, now, is Egypt rather than Assyria, and neither
Zion nor an attack upon it gets mentioned; yet the idea plainly is
part and parcel of the pattern we have been studying:

> Yahweh will strike down Egypt, healing as he strikes; then they
> will turn back to him and he will hear their prayers and heal them.

When that day comes there shall be a highway between Egypt and Assyria; Assyrians shall come to Egypt and Egyptians to Assyria; then Egyptians shall worship with Assyrians.

When that day comes Israel shall rank with Egypt and Assyria, those three, and shall be a blessing in the center of the world. So Yahweh of Hosts will bless them: A blessing be upon Egypt my people, upon Assyria the work of my hands, and upon Israel my possession.

Isaiah 19:22-25.

"Yahweh will strike, healing as he strikes." Here it becomes obvious that we are speaking of a sword *not of man*. Never could it be said of any human sword that it heals as it strikes; all it ever has done or ever can do is to destroy. And believe you me, it is a pretty fancy job of healing that Yahweh's sword can do, too. It has to be to bring about the situation that Isaiah describes: Egypt, Israel, and Assyria rooming together as buddies, and Yahweh smiling and calling them "my boys!" Truth to tell, this one is more fantastic than the one about the leopard lying down with the kid.

Isaiah sees that if ever this dream is to come to pass, it will have to be the sword of Yahweh that accomplishes it. Any attempt by man to help the surgery along with *his* sword is bound to subvert the operation. As James put it (the same James whose question launched this study): "A man's anger cannot promote the justice of God" (James 1:20). But what, then, is man's role? What is he to do? Isaiah tells us:

> Come back, keep peace, and you will be safe;
> in stillness and in staying quiet, there lies your strength.
> But you would have none of it; you said, No,
>   we will take horse and flee;
>   therefore you shall be put to flight;
>   We will ride apace;
>   therefore swift shall be the pace of your pursuers.
>   When a thousand flee at the challenge of one,
> you shall all flee at the challenge of five, until you are left
> like a pole on a mountain-top, a signal post on a hill.
> Yet Yahweh is waiting to show you his favor,
>   yet he yearns to have pity on you;

>   for Yahweh is a God of justice.
>   Happy are all who wait for him!
>   Isaiah 30:15-18.

"*Wait* for Yahweh," "come back," "keep your peace," "be still," "stay quiet"—to us, Isaiah seems to be saying that what we should do is *nothing*. That may not be quite fair to the prophet; strengthening one's relationship to God, becoming more open to him, learning to trust and obey, these certainly constitute a great deal more than doing *nothing*. At the same time, however, we need to say that Isaiah's is not the last word in this matter; in later chapters we will find some more dynamic instructions as to what men can do to help bring about God's peace.

But even so, Isaiah's is a counsel that is very much needed (and very little heeded) in our day. In contemporary peace movements—which are nothing if not *activist*—very little ever is heard about looking to God, trusting him to act, putting one's faith in his promises. Rather, the impression comes across very strongly that the accomplishment of peace must depend upon *our* wisdom, *our* strategies, *our* activism. Yet there is considerable evidence that Isaiah knew what he was talking about in suggesting that the volunteer intrusion of the sword of man (even the *pacifist* sword of man) is more likely to botch God's operation than to help it along. That would be a helpful exercise if modern peace activists would open their meetings with an appropriate reading from Isaiah.

There is one more matter regarding Isaiah to which we should give attention. Did his expectations regarding Zion work out historically? Yes and no; there isn't any other correct answer.

YES: During Isaiah's own lifetime Zion did not fall. Israel was invaded and devastated several times by the Assyrians and others. Each time, Zion and Jerusalem were spared.

NO: However, in none of these instances did the Prince of Peace appear and Zion become the center for world peace.

NO: Long after Isaiah's day, in 586 B.C., Babylonian (not Assyrian) armies invaded Israel, took Jerusalem, and made a shambles of the temple and its hilltop. God did not intervene. Later that temple was rebuilt. It was desecrated by Syrian troops in 167 B.C. but reconsecrated a few years later. Then again, in A.D. 70, Roman armies ravaged Zion. Again God did not intervene. That temple has not been rebuilt to the present day; a Moslem mosque currently occupies the site of Zion.

YES: However, if Zion be taken not so much as a particular geographical location but as the symbol of a community of those who maintain true loyalty to God, then Zion has been preserved continuously down to the present day (in either Christianity or Judaism). Indeed, Christians could maintain that Jesus' words, "Where two or three have met together in my name, I am there among them" and "On this rock I will build my church, and the powers of death shall never conquer it," are simply restatements of the old Zion promise. Further, Christians believe that the Prince of Peace has appeared, is currently on the job, and in due course will establish his Zion as the peace center of the world.

YES: Regarding the interpretation to follow, it would not be wise to try to claim that this is what Isaiah had in mind at the time he wrote; but, particularly in his analogy of the shoot growing out of the devastated stump, he comes close to casting his Zion concept into a death-and-resurrection image. It will be instructive for us to follow out the parallel.

Jesus is the one true Zion. He is Israel reduced to an absolute minimum of one faithful Israelite, the only Israelite who was completely loyal and obedient to God, completely in the image of God without anything of the universal human tendency to break that relationship. Then came God's strange work against him: he was attacked by enemies, he had to suffer for sin (not his own sin, in this case, but the sins of the rest of mankind). Finally, under the assault of Calvary, he was deserted and denied by his friends and followers, left standing alone like a pole on a mountaintop.

But in the moment of crisis, down strikes the thunderbolt of God. And in striking, it heals. The enemies have vanished. For one thing, "Zion" has escaped through death to where they can't get at him. But more, the thunderbolt has accomplished the forgiveness that removes them from the status of "enemy." In the strike, Zion's own tree was broken off; but by the power of a resurrection, a shoot comes forth. This shoot, "Zion restored," the promised Prince of Peace, lives and rules—and will live and rule "until the mountain of Yahweh's house shall be set over all other mountains," until "all the nations shall come streaming to it," until "nation shall not lift sword against nation nor ever again be trained for war."

In preparation for something we mean to do in a few chapters down the line, we need to insert a note here. In the next chapter we will introduce another Old Testament prophet who will modify significantly Isaiah's presentation of the Zion tradition. However, there are other, still later prophets who, in effect, simply redraw Isaiah's own picture. Something of this can be found in a number of the minor prophets, but the most prominent instance is the little book of Zechariah.

Zechariah's work, although written two centuries later, is little more than a re-presentation of the Isaiah scenario, making no major modifications nor introducing any particularly new elements. Zechariah's treatment is, however, more *dramatic*, using visions, esoteric symbolism, and much more spectacular imagery. Thus Zechariah's picture comes through as considerably more militaristic, savage, and bloodthirsty than Isaiah's.

Yet even so, as the counterpart of Isaiah's "sword not of man" and the stroke that heals, Zechariah has the beautiful verse, "Neither by force of arms nor by brute strength, but by my spirit" (Zechariah 4:6). We need to be alert that, in the Bible, military language, and even very warlike language, does not necessarily refer to physical, carnal combat.

But the particular point to be made here is that, by the time we get to Jesus, the Old Testament Zion tradition is much broader than just the two major prophets to whom we give detailed attention.

4

Fighting in
Reverse

Therefore will I divide him a portion with the great,
and he shall divide the spoil with the strong;
because he hath poured out his soul unto death:
and he was numbered with the transgressors;
and he bare the sin of many,
and made intercession for the transgressors.

—Deutero-Isaiah (Isaiah 53:12, KJV)

The career of our previous-chapter prophet, Isaiah, fell roughly between 742 and 700 BC, during which time Israel (Judah) was severely squeezed and dominated by the Assyrians. But after the prophet's time, the Assyrian Empire disintegrated— only to be replaced by the Babylonian Empire which rose in its stead. In 586, after a long period of threat and bullying, Babylonian armies took Jerusalem and leveled it to the ground. The populace was deported to Babylon and resettled there.

In time the Jewish situation changed. Now the great conqueror Cyrus, representative of the Persian Empire, came from the east. In the year 539, his armies took over Babylon. There he found scattered colonies of Jewish exiles whom he allowed to return home to Jerusalem—if they wanted to and could swing it financially. This offer was no big deal for Cyrus; Jerusalem was just as much under his control and within his empire as Babylon was. In one sense, it was no big deal for the Jews either; the Jerusalem to which they were free to return was nothing but a pile of rubble.

Nonetheless, over a considerable period of years, small parties of Jews did drift back and eventually were able to reconstruct something like a city with something like a temple—all, of course, as a province ruled by a governor of the Persian Empire.

Now, within the book of Isaiah is a section—chapters 40 through 55—which clearly has reference to the situation immediately preceding Cyrus's conquest of Babylon and the beginning of the return to Jerusalem. Most scholars believe that this section originated at the time and was addressed to the deportees living in Babylon—which material then got incorporated along with the work of the prophet Isaiah, who had been active approximately two centuries earlier. However, some scholars believe that the case was rather that God enabled Isaiah to see two hundred years down the line and speak as if he were present then. Although we are going to assume that the section is the work of a second prophet, one's choice of theory will not affect the basic thrust of our discussion.

We have no personal information about—not even the name of—this anonymous prophet of the exile. For the sake of convenience, he usually is referred to as "Deutero-Isaiah" (which is only a Greek way of saying "*Second* Isaiah"). For the sake of even greater convenience, we will refer to him simply as "Deutero."

It is obvious that the later prophet is familiar with the Holy War style of thinking. He can write such lines as these:

> Yahweh will go forth as a warrior,
> he will rouse the frenzy of battle like a hero;
> he will shout, he will raise the battle-cry
> and triumph over his foes.
>
> Isaiah 42:13.

It is obvious, also, that he knows the Zion tradition—and, most likely, *Isaiah's* version of that tradition. In fact, there are enough connections between the work of Deutero and Isaiah to make it likely that Deutero consciously considered himself a disciple of Isaiah and presented himself as such—which possibility would go a long way toward explaining how Deutero's work got incorporated with that of his master.

Because of the vastly different historical circumstances of Deutero's time, his version of the Zion tradition had to be greatly modified at points; and we shall note these. But where Deutero becomes most original and creative—and most contributive to our purposes—is at the point where Isaiah simply did not speak in any detail or with particular clarity.

This has to do, of course, with the means by which Yahweh turns the situation around and starts Zion on its way to becoming the world peace center. Isaiah, you will recall, made it clear that the turnabout would *not* be the result of *human* military action— "a sword not of man." Yet he very definitely did picture *God's* intervention under the figure of earthly militarism and war. And the key *person* in that event, the Prince of Peace, although the creator of everlasting peace, was presented in the guise of a conquering king.

Although he does not desert military imagery absolutely, Deutero does change this aspect of the picture in radical fashion and introduces a principle that will be determinative for our study from this point forward. Let us proceed to trace Deutero's version of the Zion story in order to discover what he does and how he does it.

Deutero, like Isaiah, knows that Yahweh has a plan for the world and that the key to the plan is Zion:

> Mark this, I have spoken, and I will bring it
>   about,
> I have a plan to carry out, and carry it out I will.

> Listen to me, all you stubborn hearts,
>   for whom victory is far off:
> I bring my victory near, it is not far off,
>   and my deliverance shall not be delayed;
> I will grant deliverance in Zion
>   and give my glory to Israel.
>
> Isaiah 46:11-13.

For Isaiah, the first step in that plan had to be Yahweh's strange work, an enemy power acting as God's agent in punishing Zion for her sin. But for Deutero, this already is done and over with; the opening words and basic theme of his great work is this announcement from God:

> Comfort, comfort my people;
>   —it is the voice of your God;
> speak tenderly to Jerusalem
>   and tell her this,
> that she has fulfilled her term of bondage,
>   that her penalty is paid;
> she has received at Yahweh's hand
>   full measure for all her sins.
>
> Isaiah 40:1-2.

Deutero is not disputing Isaiah's interpretation; he knows that Israel asked for punishment, needed punishment, and got punishment—although, in this instance, Babylon rather than Assyria was the agent. (In the following, "Jacob" is simply an alternative term, a poetic synonym for "Israel.")

> Who gave Jacob away for plunder,
>   who gave Israel away for spoil?
> Was it not Yahweh? They sinned against him,
> They would not follow his ways
>   and refused obedience to his law;
> So in his anger he poured out upon Jacob
> his wrath and the fury of battle.
>
> Isaiah 42:24-25.

Because Deutero can present the punishment as something
in the past rather than something looming up in the future, he
also can be much more positive and joyous in his approach than
Isaiah was able to be. And it must be said that, when we get to the
New Testament picture of the coming of peace, the perspective is
predominantly that of Deutero rather than Isaiah—although
without at all denying the possibility, necessity, or rightness of
punishment.

However, the holocaust through which Israel has gone
denotes not simply the punishment for sin but even more
basically a *reconciliation* with God:

> Have no fear; for I have paid the ransom;
> I have called you by name and you are my own.
> When you pass through deep waters, I am with you.
> For I am Yahweh your God,
>   the Holy One of Israel, your deliverer.
>
> Isaiah 43:1-3.

Even more, this reconciliation is made possible by the fact
that, out of his deep *love* and *grace*, Yahweh is willing to *forgive*
all of the rebellion and nastiness that Israel has handed him:

> You burdened me with your sins
>   and wearied me with your iniquities.
> I alone, I am He,
> who for his own sake wipes out your transgressions,
> who will remember your sins no more.
>
> Isaiah 43:24-25.

Here is coming to the fore a side of Yahweh's character
which simply has not been prominent in our study thus far.
Deutero is going to capitalize on it and make it the keystone of his
whole plan of peace—and the New Testament will pick it up
where he leaves off. Watch the theme develop; it is crucial.

One immediate implication can be drawn right here. There

is no possibility or hope of true and final peace for the world apart from a reconciliation with God built upon repentance for sin and a dependence upon his forgiveness and mercy. Any political program that would *build* peace in complete neglect of the God-relationship is doomed to have but partial and transitory effects at best.

With Isaiah, presumably because of the nation's sin and rebelliousness, Israel was given a largely *passive* role to play. She was to be punished and then delivered—but at every point more *acted upon* than *acting*. But Deutero opens up a new possibility: Israel has been *acted upon* by God precisely in order to prepare her *to act* as his servant.

> Remember all this, Jacob,
> remember, Israel, for you are my servant,
> I have fashioned you, and you are to serve me;
>   you shall not forget me, Israel.
> I have swept away your sins like a dissolving mist,
>   and your transgressions are dispersed like clouds;
> turn back to me; for I have ransomed you. . . .
> Yahweh has ransomed Jacob
>   and made Israel his masterpiece.
>
> Isaiah 44:21-23; cf. 41:8-9.

Neither here nor elsewhere does Deutero become specific as to what service Israel is to perform; but later we will discover that he does drop a rather large hint.

Israel's role is to be the servant of Yahweh. *Babylon's* role, Deutero sees, was the exact counterpart of what Isaiah had seen for Assyria, that is, a nation whose actions God *uses* even though he does not *approve* and which nation must then face judgment in its turn.

> When I was angry with my people,
> I dishonored my own possession

and gave them into your power [Babylon].
You showed them no mercy,
you made your yoke weigh heavy on the aged.
You said then, "I shall reign a queen forever,"
while you gave no thought to this
and did not consider how it would end.

Isaiah 47:6-7.

However, Deutero's picture also includes another foreign power, which has an entirely new and different role to play. This is the conqueror Cyrus with his Persian hordes.

Tell me, who raised up that one from the east,
one greeted by victory wherever he goes?
Who is it that puts nations into his power
and makes kings go down before him . . . ?
Whose work is this, I ask, who has brought it to
pass? . . .
It is I, Yahweh.

Isaiah 41:2-4.

Then, speaking directly *to* Cyrus, Yahweh explains his purpose:

For the sake of Jacob my servant and Israel my chosen
I have called you by name
and given you your title, though you have not known
me.

Isaiah 45:4.

He becomes more specific when speaking *about* Cyrus a few verses later:

I alone have roused this man in righteousness,
and I will smooth his path before him;
he shall rebuild my city
and let my exiles go free—
not for a price nor for a bribe,
says Yahweh of Hosts.

Isaiah 45:13.

Partly, perhaps, because his role as liberator rather than punisher of Israel is a more positive one, and partly because Deutero has hopes that in time he will come to recognize Yahweh, Cyrus comes off better in the texts than either the Assyrian or Babylonian conquerors had done earlier. Nevertheless, it clearly is stated that Cyrus does *not* know Yahweh. There is no more suggestion here than in the earlier cases that the conqueror is acting out of godly motives or that his conquests are something that God wanted. As before, they are something God can and does *use* rather than *approve*.

But because the situation is so different, the deliverance of Zion must be something quite different for Deutero from what it was for Isaiah. For Isaiah it was the last minute rescue of a Zion that was in existence although direly threatened. For Deutero it is a return to and reconstruction of a Zion which had been entirely destroyed. So Deutero reserves the best of his poetic power to describe the return to Zion:

> How beautiful upon the mountains
>   are the feet of him who brings good tidings,
> who publishes *peace*, who brings good tidings of good,
>   who publishes salvation,
>   who says to Zion, "Your God reigns."
> Hark, your watchmen lift up their voice,
>   together they sing for joy;
> for eye to eye they see
>   the return of Yahweh to Zion.

Isaiah 52:7-8, RSV; italics mine.

For Deutero, the return is the turning-point—as God's eleventh-hour intervention had been for Isaiah—and Zion again is on the way toward becoming the world peace center.

> Cry to the cities of Judah, "Your God is here."
> Here is the Lord Yahweh coming in might,
>   coming to rule with his right arm.

> His recompense comes with him,
> he carries his reward before him.
> He will tend his flock like a shepherd
> and gather them together with his arm;
> he will carry the lambs in his bosom
> and lead the ewes to water.
>
> Isaiah 40:9-11.

There is a most amazing transposition in the middle of this text, and the likelihood is that Deutero made it deliberately. The return of Yahweh to Zion with Israel in tow first is present under the military form of a conqueror returning from battle, coming in might, bringing with him the spoil. But then suddenly the figure changes to that of a shepherd with his flock, and *tenderness* becomes the dominant theme. Perhaps the prophet wants to tell us that military imagery simply isn't big enough to communicate the full significance of what is happening here. Yahweh's victorious power *and* his tender mercy go together; unless you have both, you don't have Yahweh. The gentle side of God again shows signs of coming to the fore. And it would seem proper for us to deduce that, now as then, the only hope for peace is in a faith that includes the ways of gentleness as well as those of might.

> So Yahweh's people shall come back, set free,
> and enter Zion with shouts of triumph,
> crowned with everlasting joy;
> joy and gladness shall overtake them as they come,
> and sorrowing and sighing shall flee away.
>
> Isaiah 51:11

In his picture, Deutero does not give quite the emphasis to the fact of *universal peace* that Isaiah did, but he is just as clear that the deliverance of Zion introduces a new situation and experience for the whole of mankind. It is safe to assume that the two prophets see eye to eye. However, for Deutero, it is the very event of release from exile and return to Zion that will catch the attention of the nations.

> Yahweh has bared his holy arm
>> in the sight of all nations,
> and the whole world from end to end
> shall see the deliverance of our God.
>> Isaiah 52:10.

Specifically, what they shall see in this is the "glory" of God, his wonder and goodness and love.

> Thus shall the glory of Yahweh be revealed,
> and all mankind together shall see it;
>> for Yahweh himself has spoken.
>> Isaiah 40:5.

But most important, through this seeing, the nations will be *attracted* and will themselves come to know and enjoy Yahweh.

> There is no god but me;
> there is no god other than I, victorious and able to save.
>> Look to me and be saved,
>>> you peoples from all corners of the earth;
>> for I am God, there is no other.
>> By my life I have sworn,
> I have given a promise of victory,
>> a promise that will not be broken,
> that to me every knee shall bend
>> and by me every tongue shall swear.
>> Isaiah 45:21-23.

As we have seen it thus far, Deutero's version of the Zion tradition would have to be called a *variation* of Isaiah's. For the most part, the changes seem to arise from the quite different historical situations in which the two prophets operated, although a couple of them—namely, the tender, forgiving side of Yahweh's character and Israel's call to be his servant—will have far-reaching implications.

But the one difference between Deutero and Isaiah which is truly radical, and which will prove to mark a crucial advance, concerns the person of the agent who effects the new Zion. For Isaiah, you will recall, this was the Prince of Peace, a conquering king whose victory would establish perfect peace, but whose action consistently was described under military metaphors in any case.

However, even though he stands as an exact counterpart in terms of his place in the plot, Deutero's agent is the very opposite of a conquering king; he is, indeed, "the Suffering Servant of Yahweh."

We will need to proceed with care in considering Deutero's concept of "the servant," because it turns out to be quite complex. There are a number of "servant" passages in the prophet's work. Some of them (namely, those quoted previously) clearly and explicitly identify Israel as being that one. Others, just as plainly, cannot be applied to the people Israel but must have in mind a particular individual. Still others have elements that could be taken either way or both ways.

This state of affairs ought not be attributed to confusion on Deutero's part but to the more likely possibility that he wants to speak of two different servants and at the same time point up the close relation of the two. There is the Servant Israel, and there is the Servant Individual. But the Servant Individual comes out of Israel, is himself a true Israelite, and in some ways is to represent Israel. Conversely, what the Servant Individual *is* is an ideal picture of what Servant Israel *should be;* and the service that the Servant Individual *performs* suggests the service to which Servant Israel *is called* (and thus it is that Deutero fills the gap where he failed to specify what Servant Israel is to *do*).

The strength of Deutero's presentation is that it makes plain and lucid God's method of operation at the point where Isaiah had left it somewhat ambiguous. Isaiah's Prince of Peace, recall, was to establish Zion and so launch a movement toward worldwide peace—doing this by means of a victory which at least was described in terms of earthly militarism. That is paradoxical enough in itself, but the difficulty is heightened when we realize that the Prince of Peace is pictured as an actual human king (a natural descendant of David). Try to relate that, then, to a victory won with "a sword not of man." With Deutero the picture is much sharper; let's look at it.

> Here is my servant, whom I uphold,
> my chosen one in whom I delight.
> I have bestowed my spirit upon him,
> and he will make justice shine on the nations.
> He will not call out or lift his voice high,
> or make himself heard in the open street.
> He will not break a bruised reed,
> or snuff out a smoldering wick; . . .
> he will plant justice on earth,
> while coasts and islands wait for his teaching.
> Isaiah 42:1-4.

The servant here *could* be Israel—except that neither Israel nor any other nation ever has shown an inclination to be all that quiet, modest, and unassuming. But we find an interesting juxtaposition: The task of establishing justice among the nations would sound like a job appropriate for a king, the Prince of Peace. But the *way* in which the servant goes about it is anything but kingly. Whoever heard of a king who would not make himself heard and who would be so gentle as not to break a reed hanging together by only a few tenuous fibers or to lose the spark on a wick that was sputtering its last? Kings don't get to be kings or long remain kings *that* way.

It should be pointed out, too, that few of our modern peace crusaders are this shy about making themselves heard in the open street. And those who stage escapades designed to rattle newspapers around the world hardly are modeling themselves after Deutero's servant.

> I, Yahweh, have called you with righteous purpose
> and taken you by the hand;
> I have formed you, and appointed you

> to be a light to all peoples,
> a beacon for the nations,
> to open eyes that are blind,
> to bring captives out of prison,
> out of the dungeons where they lie in darkness.
>
> Isaiah 42:6-7.

Again, these words might possibly be addressed to Israel, but they would stretch her piety beyond all reasonable expectation. Yet, "the Servant Individual *does* what the Servant Israel *should* do"; so apply the lines either way. Notice that the previous passage spoke of the servant's work of "justice," this one of "liberation." Both are essential conditions of true "peace." A mere cessation of hostilities—whether accomplished through victory, defeat, surrender, negotiation, withdrawal, or whatever—is a long way from being what the servant is out to accomplish. Our peace efforts should be every bit as broad.

> From birth Yahweh called me,
> he named me from my mother's womb.
> He made my tongue his sharp sword
> and concealed me under the cover of his hand;
> he made me a polished arrow
> and hid me out of sight in his quiver. . . .
> And now Yahweh who formed me in the womb to be his servant,
> to bring Jacob back to him
> that Israel should be gathered to him,
> now Yahweh calls me again:
> it is too slight a task for you, as my servant,
> to restore the tribes of Jacob,
> to bring back the descendants of Israel:
> I will make you a light to the nations,
> to be my salvation to earth's farthest bounds.
>
> Isaiah 49:1-2, 5-6.

The Servant himself is speaking here. It must be the Servant Individual, because it is inconceivable that Servant Israel would be called to redeem himself. However, this does not deny that the passage can have implications for Israel, also.

Our strange juxtaposition appears again. The passage opens under the military metaphors of sharp sword and polished arrow; but the quality being portrayed is *patience*—something for which swords and arrows hardly are noted. Many of our modern peace warriors hardly are noted for patience, either; in fact, some take pride in their righteous *im*patience. Nevertheless, the mark of the servant is his *patience;* even though he can't see that anything is happening, his trust in Yahweh makes him willing to lie quietly in the quiver.

The latter part of the passage emphasizes a point that was just as emphatic with Isaiah. The preservation (or in this case, restoration) of Israel (Zion) is not an end in itself for the sake simply of Israel. It is but one step in the spread of salvation "to the earth's farthest bounds." Just so, our concern dare never be merely with peace for ourselves. Until everyone has peace, no one truly has peace. The servant's ministry is universal in scope, and so must ours be.

> The Lord Yahweh has given me
> the tongue of a teacher
> and skill to console the weary
> with a word in the morning;
> he sharpened my hearing
> that I might listen like one who is taught.
> The Lord Yahweh opened my ears
> and I did not disobey or turn back in defiance.
> I offered my back to the lash,
> and let my beard be plucked from my chin,
> I did not hide my face from spitting and insult;
> but the Lord Yahweh stands by to help me;
> therefore no insult can wound me.
>   Isaiah 50:4-6.

The servant again is doing the speaking; and if it is Israel, she is claiming much more for herself than she (or any other nation) ever accomplished. The servant is a teacher—and obviously not a lay-it-to-'em lecturer but a spell-it-out-with-them counselor. He is quick to hear the word from Yahweh and skilled in transmitting it to the understanding of his hearers. And the word, from everything we are told, is that of consolation—to those who have worn themselves out in the wars and fightings of the world(?). Nothing is said here about words of chastisement and judgment.

And our modern peacemakers? How many show evidence of being all that attentive to God? And how many are committed to calm, deliberate, rational teaching? And how many are skilled "to console the weary" rather than weary any and all?

The latter part of the passage introduces what Deutero will proceed to make the central and decisive characteristic of the servant, that is, his defenselessness, his continual choice to "take it" rather than "dish it out." This one now rightfully assumes the title of the *Suffering* Servant of Yahweh. The passage immediately ahead will explain *how* his suffering works out.

Note carefully that the text says explicitly that the servant is the one who *suffers* "spitting and insult" and not the one who administers them, either in person or via placard and underground press.

And give particular attention to the last lines: "But the Lord Yahweh stands by to help me; therefore . . ." The servant does not claim that his suffering is an effective peacemaking technique in and of itself. It is only because Yahweh stands by to help that the operaton even can get off the ground. This is an idea that will be crucial for us in the pages ahead.

Our final servant passage is a long one which we will interrupt at appropriate points for comment.

> Behold, my servant shall prosper,
> he shall be lifted up, exalted to the heights.
>   Isaiah 52:13.

The end of the matter is told us at the beginning. The way of the servant will be that of offense, disrepute, humiliation, and punishment—but the end and outcome of that way is to be victory and exaltation. Deutero wants to tip us off that what we are about to witness actually is a glorious victory; we might miss it otherwise, because it surely isn't what one would look for, say, in the Prince of Peace.

> Time was when many were aghast at you, my people;
> so now many nations recoil at sight of him,
> and kings curl their lips in disgust.
> For they see what they had never been told
> and things unheard before fill their thoughts.
> Who could have believed what we have heard,
> and to whom has the power of Yahweh been revealed?
>
> Isaiah 52:14—53:1.

The scene seems to be a gathering of kings, representative of the nations of the world, who are recalling their encounter with the servant (obviously now the Servant Individual). They had judged him to be a miserable bum; but suddenly it has been revealed to them who he actually is. "Who ever would have believed that *this* character could be the one in whom the glory and power of Yahweh were being demonstrated?" These kings (nations) probably are to be thought of as the speakers of the following as well, as they contemplate the wondrous transformation that has just taken place.

> He grew up before Yahweh like a young plant
> whose roots are in parched ground;
> he had no beauty, no majesty to draw our eyes,
> no grace to make us delight in him;
> his form, disfigured, lost all the likeness of a man,
> his beauty changed beyond human semblance.
> He was despised, he shrank from the sight of men,
> tormented and humbled by suffering;
> we despised him, we held him of no account,
> a thing from which men turn away their eyes.
>
> Isaiah 53:2-3.

Deutero, rather plainly, is drawing the picture as ugly as he can. Scholars generally are agreed that the picture he has in mind is that of a leper, a victim of leprosy, a condition which, in the world of that day, would be the most repulsive and abhorrent a person could come to. And yet, even though the description focuses on how the servant *looks*, the passage would have no particular significance if it referred simply to his *physical appearance*.

More fundamentally, Deutero is speaking of the qualities of life and action that the servant represents. And the reaction of the nation-kings indicates that they see in him the very reverse of what they would expect to find in a world savior. Thus, to a very real degree, Deutero's Suffering Servant comes through as just the opposite of Isaiah's Prince of Peace; that picture of a glorious and powerful king is the first thing most people would come up with as a world savior, indeed, the very thing that world literature has produced time and time again.

What Deutero is doing in switching from the Prince of Peace to the Suffering Servant is very important, for we must keep in mind that this agent is the one through whom God wins the victory of his peaceable kingdom and that the method of the agent is therefore God's method of fighting through to that victory. What Deutero is proposing, then, is that God's method is what might be called "reverse fighting," that is, it is directly contrary to what we normally consider "fighting" to be.

Instead of power, the servant displays weakness; instead of glory, humiliation; instead of public acclaim, social rejection; instead of assertive thrusts against the enemy, absorption of the enemy's thrusts against him; instead of making the enemy suffer, suffering himself.

Although it will be difficult for us to understand it so, this is a method of *fighting*, that is, it is a means by which God truly does win the victory and get his will to be done. As the nation-kings continue to speak, Deutero explains a little as to *how* reverse fighting works.

> Yet on himself he bore our sufferings,
> our torments he endured,
> while we counted him smitten by God,
> struck down by disease and misery;
> but he was pierced for our transgressions,
> tortured for our iniquities;
> the chastisement he bore is health for us
> and by his scourging we are healed.
> We had all strayed like sheep,
> each of us had gone his own way;
> but Yahweh laid upon him
> the guilt of us all.
>
> Isaiah 53:4-6.

The suffering of the servant, we now discover, is what technically is known as "vicarious suffering." "Vicarious" comes from a Latin word meaning "substituting"; and "vicarious suffering" is that which one voluntarily takes upon himself in order that it will not have to be suffered by the one who actually deserves it and has brought it to pass. Previously the nation-kings had despised the servant because they thought he was being punished for his own wickedness; suddenly they have realized that the suffering is that which belongs to *them* but which he has offered to bear so that they will not have to bear it. While they had been hating him, he had been doing the most loving thing possible for them. "By *his* scourging *we* are healed." And thus we find some sense behind Isaiah's reference to the stroke of Yahweh that heals as it strikes (see pages 83-84).

> He was afflicted, he submitted to be struck down
> and did not open his mouth;
> he was led like a sheep to the slaughter,
> like a ewe that is dumb before the shearers.
> Without protection, without justice, he was taken away;
> and who gave a thought to his fate,
> how he was cut off from the world of living men,
> stricken to the death for my people's transgression?
> He was assigned a grave with the wicked,

> a burial-place among the refuse of mankind,
> though he had done no violence
> and spoken no word of treachery.
> > Isaiah 53:7-9.

How does the servant suffer? Quietly: without calling attention to himself, without theatricals. (With the assistance of the press and broadcasting media, ours certainly has become the age of theatrical martyrdoms.) Quietly: without making any attempt to play up the injustice that was being done to him. The persecutors made the discovery of this injustice for themselves—undoubtedly with greater effect than if the servant had tried to point it out to them. Quietly: without complaint, protest, or accusation either to God or to the persecutors.

How long, or to what extent, is he willing to suffer in silence? Unto death—and not "unto" in the sense that stops short *at the point of death* but in a sense that accepts death itself as a part of that vicarious suffering.

The servant's death is crucial to an understanding of what is transpiring through his suffering. In and through that suffering, of course, the enemy nation-kings are reconciled, they find God, and the conflict comes to an end. However, it is not as though vicarious suffering were a *technique* which just anyone can decide to use and with it conquer his enemies and win the day for righteousness. After all, the servant winds up dead; and that is no very good reconciliation that eliminates one of the parties. Vicarious suffering "works" only when God himself is in the action and because *he* has the power to bring victory out of defeat.

> Yet Yahweh took thought for his tortured servant
> and healed him who had made himself a sacrifice for sin;
> so shall he enjoy long life and see his children's children,
> > and in his hand Yahweh's cause shall prosper.
> After all his pains he shall be bathed in light,
> after his disgrace he shall be fully vindicated;
> so shall he, my servant, vindicate many,
> himself bearing the penalty of their guilt.
> > Isaiah 53:10-11.

At this point, Deutero's language is not absolutely clear and explicit. What is plain is that the event goes beyond simply the servant's action and requires the complement of Yahweh's own direct action in healing and vindication. A resurrection or something of the sort would seem to be about the only possibility. But in any case, the servant had volunteered for suffering and death in obedience to God, trusting that God could and would act so as to use the obedience for good. God did act; and in the combined actions of the servant and God, the servant was vindicated and, along with him, those in whose behalf he had suffered.

> Therefore I will allot him a portion with the great,
>   and he shall share the spoil with the mighty,
> because he exposed himself to face death
>   and was reckoned among transgressors,
> because he bore the sin of many
>   and interceded for their transgressions.
>
> Isaiah 53:12.

With this conclusion, Deutero has brought us full circle. He is back to military, Holy War language, describing the reward of a conqueror. The servant shall be honored in the hall of fame along with the great kings and heroes; he shall receive his share of the spoils he has taken. And how did he merit this honor? By pursuing the enemy to the death? No; by exposing *himself* to death! By asserting his righteousness over the transgressors? No; by *himself* being reckoned among the transgressors! By visiting the sins of the wicked upon their heads? No; by *himself* bearing their sins and interceding for them! There is no doubt but that Deutero wants as powerfully as possible to express the paradox of "reverse fighting" in this verse: the way of the servant is just the opposite of what we call "fighting," yet the "victory" is real victory in every sense of the word.

It is clear that Isaiah's Prince of Peace is patterned on the model of an Israelite king; he is the ideal king. Likewise, scholars are convinced that Deutero's Suffering Servant is patterned on the model of an Israelite *prophet;* he is the ideal prophet.

Now Christians, of course, inevitably see *both* of these pictures pointing to and being fulfilled in Jesus Christ. However, it is not all that clear that the two prophets themselves understood that their respective visions had a common focus. From all we know about the Jewish tradition from the time of the prophets until the time of Christ, it seems not to have occurred to anyone that these two pictures *could* be related. It is only the *fact* of Jesus Christ that *provides* the focus. Jesus, as it were, set out to pull the two lines into himself; he acts in such a way that the early Christians, for the first time, can see that both are applicable to him.

It takes some interpretive work to make that happen. Isaiah's conquering king is used to identify Christ's *office* and Deutero's suffering servant to describe the *content* or *means* by which he fulfilled the office. In the process, Isaiah's figure must be spiritualized or deliteralized, for obviously Jesus did not come as an actual, earthly king or win his victory in the way that such kings do.

And yet perhaps the prophets themselves have given us license for making this very move. Isaiah, even though portraying a very down-to-earth, military-type, kingly conqueror, still wanted to talk about "a sword not of man" and a kind of victory that would establish universal peace and brotherhood (which Isaiah plainly did not believe that any human military action could accomplish). And Deutero, while portraying a most unmilitary figure, still insisted on sneaking bits of kingly-military imagery into his description.

However, there is more that should be said. We must recognize that Deutero mentions "reverse fighting" only in connection with this special agent of Yahweh's who is the Servant Individual. "Reverse fighting" clearly is the method God means to use in the special case of his *final* victory, but Deutero does not apply the method any more broadly than that; he nowhere instructs or even hints to his hearers that *they* are to practice the method. Yet maybe he does! Recall that his picture includes Servant Israel as well as Servant Individual and that the two deliberately are written so as to be very closely related and even overlapping. Yet we are given actually no insight as to what the particular role and procedures of Servant Israel are to be. Is there any other conclusion to draw but that Servant Israel is to be engaged *with* Servant Individual in *his* mission?

Did Deutero's ideas work out historically? Yes and no; there isn't any other correct way to answer. YES: Deutero saw accurately that Cyrus of Persia would conquer Babylon and release the Jewish exiles to return to Jerusalem. There was a return. NO: That return did not prove to be a great and glorious event that caught the attention of the nations, turned them to God, and put history on a new course. In actuality, it was a very ordinary, undramatic, rather shabby occurrence. Further, although Israel did keep the faith alive, compile the Old Testament scriptures, and make an inestimable contribution to the world, the quality of her servanthood to Yahweh remained the so-so thing it always had been. And of course, the Servant Individual failed to appear as part of the whole complex of events surrounding the return from exile, as Deutero apparently expected he would.

But YES: As we found to be true with *Isaiah's* vision, the fact that things did not work out just in the way and at the time the prophet anticipated does not mean that his was not true insight. Our story isn't over yet, nor have we heard the last of Deutero's ideas.

As with the case of the previous chapter, this one also calls for a footnote to prepare us for future exigencies. We have developed Deutero's version of the Zion tradition using material from Isaiah 40-55. However, the book of Isaiah also includes material chaptered 56-66. Scholars can't agree whether this part of the text is the work of Deutero, partly by Deutero, by a third prophet to be known as Trito-Isaiah, or by a miscellany of later writers. Because we didn't need to use the material for what we were doing, we chose not to become involved. However, a quick look will provide us a contribution for our *next* topic.

Isaiah 55-66 is deeply informed by Zion-tradition ideas and language, although in a style more reminiscent of Isaiah than Deutero. No hint of voluntary, vicarious suffering appears at all; and there is but little that points to the concept of servant. There is more of and a tougher brand of Holy War language than even Isaiah used.

Thus there is the familiar idea of a last-minute intervention to save Zion—but with a difference (at least in tone).

> Yahweh saw, and in his eyes it was an evil thing,
> > that there was no justice;
> > he saw that there was no man to help
> > and was outraged that no one intervened;
> > so his own arm brought him victory
> > and his own integrity upheld him.
> > He put on integrity as a coat of mail
> > and the helmet of salvation on his head;
> > he put on garments of vengeance
> > and wrapped himself in a cloak of jealous anger.
> > High God of retribution that he is,
> > > he pays in full measure,
> > wreaking his anger on his foes, retribution on his enemies.
> > So from the west men shall fear his name,
> > > fear his glory from the rising of the sun;
> > for it shall come like a shining river,
> > the spirit of Yahweh hovering over it,
> > come as the ransomer of Zion.
> > > > > > > Isaiah 59:15-20.

Likewise, the idea of redeemed Zion attracting the nations to herself again is clearly stated:

> Arise, Jerusalem,
> rise clothed in light; your light has come
> > and the glory of Yahweh shines over you.
> For, though darkness covers the earth
> > and dark night the nations,

> Yahweh shall shine upon you
> and over you shall his glory appear;
> and the nations shall march towards your light
> and their kings to your sunrise.
>
> Isaiah 60:1-3.

But in this case the text goes on to describe Israel lording it over these nations and making slaves of them.

However, the most important passage out of these chapters is the description of a servant-type figure, even though he is not identified as "servant." It would seem to be an enlargement based upon Deutero's lines: "I have bestowed my spirit upon him . . . to open eyes that are blind, to bring captives out of prison" (Isaiah 42:1, 7). It reads:

> The spirit of the Lord Yahweh is upon me
> because Yahweh has anointed me;
> he has sent me to bring good news to the humble,
>   to bind up the broken-hearted,
> to proclaim liberty to captives
>   and release to those in prison;
> to proclaim a year of Yahweh's favor
>   and a day of the vengeance of our God.
>
> Isaiah 61:1-2.

It should be noted both that the concluding line above hardly is commensurate with what we found in Deutero and that, when this passage is quoted in the New Testament, it stops short of that line.

Before we leap across into the New Testament, let's take a look at where we've come. Genesis showed us that wars and fightings come about because man decided to quit fighting along with Yahweh in a ballerina posture and instead to fight it in his own way and for his own end, which is the construction of security for himself. Joshua-Judges taught us that the only cure is for man to make the determined and disciplined effort to join Yahweh in his war and let him call the shots. It went on to portray a sincere and honest effort at doing this—which effort, even so, was destined to fall short.

Isaiah spoke to that failure by pointing out that man has so perverted himself that his ways of fighting simply are incapable of serving God's battle plan. And finally, Deutero came in to tell us that God's *method* of fighting is different from what we have been considering and thus opens again the possibility that man might have a role to play after all.

Each step of the argument from Genesis to Deutero-Isaiah required the existence of all the prior steps as truths upon which to build. At the same time, each step has called for another step above in order to complete its truth. Our next step, as we move into the New Testament, will be from *theory* to *actuality*, from *promise* to *fulfillment*.

5

The Victory of
Skull Hill

On that cross he despoiled the cosmic powers and authorities, and boldly made a spectacle of them, leading them as captives in his triumphal procession.
                                        —Colossians 2:15

This chapter—which represents the heart of our argument—treats the *history* of Jesus, particularly his death and resurrection. The following chapter, a comparatively short and easy one, will treat Jesus' *teachings* concerning war and peace. The sequence likely will strike any thinking reader as being completely wrong-headed both as to chronology and emphasis—but this is the way we are going to do it.

"But obviously Jesus did his teaching *before* he was crucified or resurrected!"

Yes, obviously; there's no argument on that point. But what we have in the New Testament is not simply and directly "Jesus' teaching." What we have are early Christian *presentations* of Jesus' teachings. And at every point they are *presented* as the teachings of God's Christ, the Lord who died and was resurrected. The interest of the New Testament writers consistently is *first* in *who* is this Jesus whose history is recounted and only then in *what* were his teachings.

"But the Christian peace position is based on Jesus' *teachings*, and that is where the major emphasis should fall."

Perhaps; but even though many books suggest otherwise, I don't think so. Go that way and Jesus tends to be seen simply as a great ethical teacher, one of whose ethical teachings happens to be that of *peace*. But the sad truth is that ethical teachings are what we (Christians as well as non-Christians) are best at picking and choosing among according to our own preferences; and ethical teachings are what we are most adept at explaining away when they do not suit our preferences. But go the way we have chosen and one hardly can reject the peace position without rejecting the gospel itself. And as a happy consequence, Jesus' teachings of the next chapter become as plain and inevitable as the study of human physiology plainly and inevitably leads to the teaching that one ought to keep breathing if he wants to stay alive.

You are free to skip ahead and read the next chapter first if you want to, but it won't make much sense that way.

The thesis of this chapter is that the Old Testament Holy War/Zion tradition provides *the* framework within which the New Testament Christians found their understanding of the history of Jesus, his death and resurrection. This is the framework within which they found their understanding of what God did do, is doing, and will do through Christ and for the world.

In one respect, then, our perspective is changed radically from what it was in earlier chapters. There it was *promise;* here it is *fulfillment.* There it was *projection*—projection taking into account what were at that time current situations and alignments but still dealing essentially with what it was hoped might happen in the future. Here it is *interpretation* and *application,* discovering the reality and meaning of accomplished facts and events actually in process. The most significant feature of the New Testament presentation is the announcement, "It's happening!" Or as it is put in the Gospel of Matthew:

> But happy are your eyes because they see, and your ears because
> they hear! Many prophets and saints, I tell you, desired to see what
> you now see, yet never saw it; to hear what you hear, yet never
> heard it.
> Matthew 13:16-17.

And still, even more than simple application is involved; to
say merely that Jesus *fulfills* the Zion tradition doesn't get to the
heart of the matter. Even earlier we have seen how the tradition
had to grow and undergo modification in order to accommodate
new revelation and insight. Likewise, the *events* of Jesus' history
were great enough that even the glorious promises of the older
tradition had to be stretched mightily if they were to do justice to
what was taking place. It is to this revamping that we will give
particular attention.

However, our treatment will not pretend to be a work of
technical Bible scholarship. If such were the case, then regarding
any bit of evidence cited from one of the Gospels, for instance, the
question would need to be asked, "Whose thinking does this
represent: Jesus'? that of the early tradition underlying the
Gospel? the Gospel writer's himself?" But although we firmly are
convinced that some of our evidence indicates that it was Jesus
himself who started the process of interpreting his history according to the Zion tradition, we will investigate only far enough to
claim that it was being done in New Testament times regardless
of who was doing it. Similarly, in dealing with the Pauline literature, we will lump it all together and call the author "Paul"
without venturing into the knotty problems of who wrote what
when.

Finally, we will not make an effort to cite all the evidence
that is present. We will be quite selective, using only that which
contributes to important patterns of thought, marks a significant
modification of the previous understanding, or is particularly appropriate to our quest regarding peace. We are not so much
interested in proving a thesis as in opening up a path of interpretation.

The primary and crucial move in the New Testament is the amalgamation of Deutero's Suffering Servant with Isaiah's Prince of Peace. As we saw, the prophets themselves had somewhat pointed things in this direction. However, as we also noted earlier, the two figures are diverse enough in character that apparently it never occurred to Jewish thinkers that the two could go together.

Yet it is misleading to imply that the New Testament tradition performed the amalgamation as a deliberate and self-conscious bringing together of two separate strands of thought; rather, it simply was assumed that the Old Testament prophets had had in mind a Servant Messiah all along. This becomes particularly apparent in Luke-Acts (the Gospel of Luke and the book of Acts are two volumes of one work written by one author, and we will treat them as a unity). At four or five different points in that work, reference is made to the prophets after the manner of this instance:

> This is how God fulfilled what he had foretold in the utterances of all the prophets: that his Messiah should suffer. Repent then and turn to God, so that your sins may be wiped out. Then the Lord may grant you a time of recovery and send you the Messiah he has already appointed, that is, Jesus. He must be received into heaven until the time of universal restoration comes, of which God spoke by his holy prophets.
>
> Acts 3:18-21.

This passage is shot through with Zion concepts. And in the New Testament, now, the term "Messiah" (Christ)—and on occasion "Son of Man"—denotes a figure that combines elements from Isaiah and Deutero.

The combination represents a radical departure from earlier thought; and yet it was made so easily. In part, this must be attributed to the fact that early Christian thinkers just did not make the sort of historical, developmental distinctions with which we have been dealing. They gave no thought to the difference between Isaiah, Deutero-Isaiah, or the third part of Isaiah. In fact,

they gave little or no thought to the difference between one prophetic book and another. A not at all uncommon occurrence in
the New Testament is to find an author saying, "As it is written in
the prophets," and giving a quotation that is constructed out of
lines taken from a number of different prophets. However, the
significant point is that, no matter *how* the New Testament
writers quote the Old Testament, the passages to which they go
almost invariably represent the Zion tradition.

What we are dealing with, then, is plainly a Holy War/Zion
tradition and yet one that is somewhat different from anything
that had gone before—just as the Mississippi River is quite a different river below its confluence with the Missouri, the Illinois,
and the Ohio from what it is above, even though the lower
Mississippi still is identified and used simply as "the Mississippi"
rather than as "the Missouri-Illinois-Ohio-Mississippi."

But why were the New Testament Christians able to accept
as obvious a confluence which their Jewish forebears hadn't even
seen as possible? Were the Christians all that much smarter? Not
at all. The difference is that the history of Jesus revealed the possibility—and the actuality—of a confluence that wasn't even
guessed otherwise. And this characterizes the nature of the relationship all the way through. The Zion tradition is not taken as a
static given and then the history of Jesus tortured to conform to it.
Rather, the history of Jesus is the given, and the Zion tradition
then is used to interpret it, even when the Zion tradition must be
stretched and modified in the process.

The Zion tradition serves the Christian gospel in some ways
that are so basic as to be presuppositions that need not be proved
and only with difficulty *could* be proved with specific quotations.
For example, harking back to our chapters on Genesis and Joshua-
Judges, the New Testament assumes at every point that Jesus
plays the perfect ballerina to God the Father. Consequently,
whatever Jesus does in the way of fighting is *the* definition of
what Holy War truly is. The Joshua-Judges understanding must

be measured against Jesus rather than vice versa.

W. D. Davies argues that the basic New Testament term "gospel" (good news) probably roots back into Isaiah 52:7 *ff.* (see page 95 above). Thus, for the early Christians, the word referred to the good news of God's conquest in behalf of Zion through which he establishes the new order of peace and justice. The very word "gospel," then, is a fruit of the Zion tradition.

Likewise, the concept "kingdom of God"—which all of our sources agree lay at the core of Jesus' preaching, teaching, and activity—seems clearly to be the equivalent of the Zion picture of a coming era of worldwide recognition of Yahweh with its attendant blessings of peace, harmony, and prosperity. The New Testament picture is not drawn in as narrowly geographical, political, materialistic terms as is the prophets' picture; but there would seem to be no doubt but that the one is based upon the other.

Nevertheless, the Zion tradition comes to view most particularly as the framework for interpreting Jesus' *death and resurrection;* and its contribution in this regard is of crucial importance.

The New Testament also provides some other models for understanding the death and resurrection. These can be grouped as what might be called "individualist-atonement" models. They include: (1) The Sacrifice Model. This one roots in the Old Testament cult, the liturgical tradition of animal sacrifice, and understands Jesus' death as a sacrifice made for the expiation of sin. (2) The Redemption Model. This one derives from the legal practice by which a slave was purchased from his owner in order to be set free. Jesus' death is understood as a ransom payment that buys the sinner's freedom. (3) The Justification Model. This one assumes a courtroom setting and understands Jesus' death as an action that wins from the judge an acquittal for the defendant.

These models are to be found in the Scriptures, and we have no desire to deny either their existence or their value. However, a reading of the New Testament as a whole makes it plain that the Zion model is used much more extensively and pervasively than any of the other three—or all three of them put together. Besides, the Zion model carries some theological advantages that the others simply do not possess.

The individualist-atonement models tend to present Jesus' work exclusively in terms of a one-to-one transaction, the focus coming to be on what he has done *for me*. The Zion model does not deny the individual aspect ("he was pierced for our [my] transgressions") but goes on to recognize that the Messiah's victory also includes the nations and leads even to a transformed world.

The individualist-atonement models tend to center on just two historical moments, namely, Jesus' death and the believer's faith acceptance of its benefit. The Zion model deals with a historical continuum that includes the entire history of Jesus, his present lordship, and what is yet to happen through him.

The individualist-atonement models present an action that is complete and finished in itself. The Zion model also points to more that is to come.

The individualist-atonement models focus on Jesus' death and do not suggest any *necessary* reason for his resurrection (although, of course, they do not *deny* it). The Zion model makes the resurrection just as necessary as and entirely inseparable from the crucifixion.

The individualist-atonement models picture the believer as a passive recipient of Jesus' work. The Zion model enlists him as part of the action.

And finally—but very important for our purposes—the individualist-atonement models have no particular implications concerning world peace and our responsibilities in that regard. The Zion model very definitely does.

With its emphasis on the vicarious suffering of the Servant, the Zion model cannot be said to lack anything that the other models provide; and it includes a great deal that we would be much poorer without. How unfortunate, then, that, for some reason or other, Christian doctrine since the time of the New

Testament has tended to go exclusively with the individualist-atonement models and has pretty much lost sight of the Zion model. The New Testament itself strikes a much better balance; and our study marks an effort to move back toward that balance.

As we launch an examination of some texts, recall that we are not attempting to collect all appropriate evidence. If some books do not get used at all, it is not because they are lacking in Zion references but because we have chosen to present the major line of thought from other material. We begin with Luke-Acts.

Through the opening chapters of his Gospel, which deal with the impending birth of Jesus, Luke, through the mouth of one person and another, presents a considerable amount of *hymnic* material. This seems to be consciously in the style of the Old Testament prophetic writings; and Holy War, Zion ideas figure very prominently. The character of these passages would indicate that Luke deliberately wants to build a bridge from the Old Testament Zion tradition to the story he is about to tell. We quote some of the most impressive lines from these hymns.

> He will be great; he will bear the title "Son of the Most High"; the Lord God will give him the throne of his ancestor David, and he will be king over Israel for ever; his reign shall never end.
>
> Luke 1:32-33.

> The deeds [God's] own right arm has done
>   disclose his might:
> the arrogant of heart and mind he has put to rout,
> he has brought down monarchs from their thrones,
>   but the humble have been lifted high.
> The hungry he has satisfied with good things,
>   the rich sent empty away.
>
> Luke 1:51-53.

> Praise to the God of Israel!
> For he has turned to his people, saved them and set
>   them free,

and has raised up a deliverer of victorious power
    from the house of his servant David.
So he promised . . .
that he would deliver us from our enemies, . . .
and grant us, free from fear, to worship him
    with a holy worship, with uprightness of heart,
    in his presence, our whole life long. . . .
For in the tender compassion of our God
    the morning sun from heaven will rise upon us,
to shine on those who live in darkness, under the cloud
      of death,
    and to guide our feet into *the way of peace*.
                    Luke 1:68-79; italics mine.

Now thy promise is fulfilled.
For I have seen with my own eyes
the deliverance which thou has made ready in full view
    of all the nations:
a light that will be a revelation to the heathen,
    and a glory to thy people Israel.
                  Luke 2:29-32.

Much of the phraseology above is, of course, very reminiscent of the Old Testament and particularly Isaiah. Most of the elements of the Zion pattern are present—the exception being any hint of the Suffering Servant. However, this can be only because Luke is saving it for later; recall that our mention of the prophets being quoted to the effect that the Messiah must suffer was in special reference to Luke-Acts.

Luke 4:16-21 is a key scene which the author clearly means to present as the introduction and theme statement of Jesus' public ministry. The Master attends synagogue and reads from the scroll of Isaiah. The passage as Luke quotes it actually is a combination of lines from Isaiah 61 and 42 (see pp. 111 and 99-100 above) describing the Servant's *service* although not his *suffering*. Jesus concludes, "Today in your very hearing this text has come true." There is not the slightest doubt that, for Luke at least, the good works of Jesus were to be understood as the Servant doing his serving.

Luke's twenty-first chapter is an interesting one. Jesus is speaking of the end of the age, the close of history which often is referred to as "the second coming." The pattern, indisputably, is that of the Zion tradition:

> When you hear of wars and insurrections, do not fall into panic. . . .
> Nation will make war upon nation, kingdom upon kingdom . . . .
> But before all this happens they will set upon you and persecute
> you. You will be brought before synagogues and put in prison; you
> will be haled before kings and governors for your allegiance to
> me. . . . Even your parents and brothers, your relations and friends,
> will betray you. . . . But when you see Jerusalem encircled by
> armies, then you may be sure that her destruction is near. . . . There
> will be great distress in the land and a terrible judgment upon this
> people. . . . Jerusalem will be trampled down by foreigners until
> their day has run its course. . . . And then they will see the Son of
> Man coming on a cloud with great power and glory. When all this
> begins to happen, stand upright and hold your heads high, because
> your liberation is near.
>
> Luke 21:9-28.

Here is a full-fledged Zion cycle which includes Zion devastated by the nations and delivered through a last minute intervention involving the Messiah. There is also here an element which we have not met before but which soon will become very familiar, namely, Servant Israel (i.e., the *new* Israel which is the Christian community) suffering after the likeness of the Servant Individual.

We discover that both Jesus' earthly history and his final, eschatological history are to be understood in terms of the Zion tradition. In this regard, it is interesting to discover that Matthew includes some of the same words of Jesus quoted here but in a completely different context. In Matthew, Jesus speaks them to his disciples as part of his instructions for their immediate mission and ministry even before his death and resurrection.

In his next chapter, the account of the last supper, Luke includes more of a Suffering Servant emphasis than does any other Gospel writer:

> In the world, kings lord it over their subjects; and those in authority
> are called their country's "Benefactors." Not so with you: on the
> contrary, the highest among you must bear himself like the young-
> est, the chief of you like a servant. For who is greater—the one who
> sits at table or the servant who waits on him? Surely the one who sits
> at table. Yet here am I among you like a servant. You are the men
> who have stood firmly by me in my times of trial; and now I vest in
> you the kingship which my Father vested in me; you shall eat and
> drink at my table in my kingdom and sit on thrones as judges of the
> twelve tribes of Israel.
>
> Luke 22:25-30.

(And a few verses later, Luke has Jesus quote a line from
Deutero's vicarious suffering passage and apply it to himself.)

Here we have a clear statement of the "reverse fighting"
principle ("not so with you"), explicit servant language, a servant
to be exalted to "kingship," and the suggestion that Servant Israel
is to recapitulate the experience of Servant Individual. How
Zionish can you get?

(The Gospel of John is not nearly as much informed by the
Zion tradition as are the other Gospels, but there are spots. One of
these is the last supper. You will recall that in place of any account
of the bread and cup, John has Jesus washing the feet of his disciples and instructing them to wash one another's feet. The Lord's
Supper, for John, consists of a graphic servant [even *suffering*
servant] symbol—and that symbol also signifies that Servant Israel is to share the mission of Servant Individual.)

Near the close of his Gospel, Luke has the risen Jesus interpret his own death and resurrection by referring to the Zion
tradition:

> "How dull you are! . . . How slow to believe all that the prophets
> said! Was the Messiah not bound to suffer thus before entering
> upon his glory?" Then he began with Moses and all the prophets,
> and explained to them the passages which referred to himself in
> every part of the scriptures.
>
> Luke 24:25-27.

As he moves, then, into Acts, Luke opens on a very appropriate note. The disciples ask Jesus, "Lord, is this the time when you are to establish once again the sovereignty of Israel?" These men know their Zion cycle well enough to know what ought to come next. After the catastrophic intervention that delivers Zion and exalts the Messiah from suffering servanthood to kingship (Jesus' death and resurrection, of course), Israel is to be restored and set up as the world peace center. And Jesus' answer to the disciples, by the way, is not "You've got it all wrong," but "Be patient; all in due time."

However, in the early chapters of Acts, Luke apparently intends to build a bridge after the manner in which he opened his Gospel. The building, this time, is of *sermonic* rather than hymnic material; and it is quite different in that it is intended to bridge, not from the prophets to the history of Jesus, but from the history of Jesus to the life of the church. Several instances of the preaching of the apostles are recorded, predominantly from the mouth of Peter; and the Zion tradition provides the theme.

We quoted one example from this preaching in a different connection (see page 116 above).   Here is another:

> They did indeed make common cause in this very city against thy holy servant Jesus whom thou didst anoint as Messiah. Herod and Pontius Pilate conspired with the Gentiles and the people of Israel to do all the things which, under thy hand and by thy decree, were foreordained. And now, O Lord, mark their threats, and enable thy servants to speak thy word with all boldness. Stretch out thy hand to heal and cause signs and wonders to be done through the name of thy holy servant Jesus.
>
> Acts 4:27-30.

This prayer explicitly identifies Jesus as the servant become Messiah. It makes a reference which undoubtedly intends the Old Testament Zion tradition ("foreordained by thy decree"). It also petitions that the Servant's ministry be continued through Servant Israel.

> Peter replied for himself and the apostles: "We must obey God rather than men. The God of our fathers raised up Jesus whom you had done to death by hanging him on a gibbet. He it is whom God has exalted with his own right hand as leader and savior, to grant Israel repentance and forgiveness of sins.
>
> Acts 5:29-31.

Here we encounter a couple of themes that are central to our study, although they receive particular mention only now. The ultimate suffering of the Servant is, of course, his death on the cross; the act of God that exalts him to kingship is, of course, his resurrection. Throughout the New Testament—unlike much modern preaching and teaching—the resurrection is given at least equal billing with the cross; indeed, as two elements of the one act of deliverance, they are so closely tied together that they cannot get out of balance. Consistently, too, the New Testament identifies *God* as the performer of the resurrection ("the sword not of man that heals as it strikes") rather than describing the event as something that happened of itself out of the inherent power and goodness of Jesus.

In the second place, this passage recognizes—with Deutero—that he was pierced for our transgressions, i.e., the purpose behind the Servant's death and exaltation is that we might find repentance and forgiveness of sins. However, in Deutero's vicarious-suffering chapter the kings who had inflicted the suffering discovered for themselves that it was *their* transgressions he bore. In the New Testament preaching, however, the kings—and all the people they represent—are *told* of their guilt. There is, of course, no slighting of the proclamation that through his suffering they are offered *forgiveness* for that guilt; but nevertheless there is a strong emphasis—as it appears here—that *"you* did him to death by hanging him on a gibbet."

In Acts 8, Philip comes upon a traveler who is reading Deutero's vicarious-suffering chapter and not making a great deal of sense out of it. Philip explains it by telling him "the good news of Jesus."

Finally, in Acts 13, Luke gives us a long sermon by Paul.
Boiled down, it is seen to be an eloquent exposition of the Zion
tradition:

> This is the man from whose posterity God, as he promised, has
> brought Israel a savior, Jesus. . . . The people of Jerusalem and their
> rulers did not recognize him, or understand the words of the
> prophets which are read Sabbath by Sabbath; indeed they fulfilled
> them by condemning him. . . . We are here to give you the good
> news that God, who made the promise to the fathers, has fulfilled it
> for the children by raising Jesus from the dead. . . . It is through
> him that forgiveness of sins is now being proclaimed to you.
>
> Acts 13:23, 27, 32-33, 38-39.

With his sermon collection in early Acts, Luke has bridged
beautifully from the history of Jesus to the life of the church; and
the stuff of his bridge is the Zion cycle.

Luke makes one further use of the Zion tradition that is both
important and interesting. At that point in the Acts account where
the church is struggling over the question of whether the gospel of
Jesus should be offered to the Gentiles (the nations), the Zion
tradition is brought in to support the move.

> It was necessary that the word of God should be declared to you
> [Jews] first. But since you reject it and thus condemn yourselves as
> unworthy of eternal life, we now turn to the Gentiles. For these are
> our instructions from the Lord: "I have appointed you to be a light
> for the Gentiles, and a means of salvation to earth's farthest
> bounds."
>
> Acts 13:46-48.

The quotation, of course, is straight out of a Servant passage
from Deutero-Isaiah. And two chapters later, when the so-called
Council of Acts 15 is convened at Jerusalem to establish an official
church policy on the matter, the chairman James bases the decision upon another Zion quote from the prophets, this one
constructed out of lines taken from different places:

Thereafter I will return and rebuild the fallen house of David; even from its ruins I will rebuild it, and set it up again, that they may seek the Lord—all the rest of mankind, and the Gentiles, whom I have claimed for my own.
                                                            Acts 15:16-17

Here, then, we see that the Christian concept of the brotherhood of man, the promise of universal restoration, world-wide peace and reconciliation—these all are derived directly from the Old Testament Zion tradition. And note carefully one aspect of the matter: This human brotherhood is not understood as something that exists by nature or into which the race, on its own, gradually will evolve. No, this brotherhood is a deliberate creation of God, accomplished through the work of his Messiah, his Suffering-Servant Messiah. And the good news of the gospel is that this Servant already has suffered, that he *has* been installed as Messiah, and that his work of universal restoration is in progress.

The Gospel of Matthew also leans strongly upon the Zion tradition and applies it to the history of Jesus in some important ways that we do not find in Luke-Acts.

This author, in Matthew 12:15-21, also uses a quotation from Deutero as the means of confirming and typifying Jesus' servant ministry; but he picks a different passage from the one Luke did. Luke, recall, used the one about proclaiming release for prisoners and recovery of sight for the blind. Matthew uses the one about establishing justice even though not raising one's voice in the street (see page 99 above).

Matthew makes a particularly important contribution in describing the events of Holy Week. He recounts the same incidents that the other Gospels do; and those authors may have had in mind the same interpretation. However, Matthew makes that interpretation much more clear and explicit.

And because this is so, we now interrupt our investigation strictly of Matthew to look at the Holy Week sequence as such—

giving our attention to the pattern of *the events themselves* without particular regard to any one Gospel writer's reporting and interpreting of them. This will enable us to discover something very important.

No biblical scholar would try to deny the truth of what we have been noting, namely, that the New Testament presentation and interpretation of Jesus is shot through with Zion-tradition references, even to the actual quoting of Isaiah and Deutero. But what many of these scholars do deny is that this evidence in any way demonstrates that *Jesus himself* understood *his own* career and ministry in these terms. They take the Zion material as marking a *post-Easter* development, a thought contribution made by the early Christian tradition and the Gospel writers themselves. In response, I am proposing that the Holy Week sequence firmly establishes Jesus himself as the one who made the original application of the Zion tradition and that the Christians of the post-Easter development were merely following *his* lead.

Scholars long have recognized that what we are calling "the Holy Week sequence" constitutes a unique resource regarding the history of Jesus. Up to this point in their accounts, the four Gospels show considerable freedom and lack of coordination among themselves; they cannot be made to produce a clear and unmistakable chronology of where Jesus went and what he did when. Yet suddenly, with the advent of Holy Week, all that changes; now *all four* of the accounts (including the Gospel of John, which otherwise almost never coordinates with the Synoptics) come into remarkable agreement as to what major events took place in what order. However, with their accounts of *Easter*, it must be recognized, this Gospel coordination is lost; each goes back to its differing version of things.

But what this means is that the portion of the story of Jesus of which we can be most certain—the place where we can speak with the greatest *historical* assurance—is that, during the last week of his life, Jesus went through the sequence of (a) triumphal entry into Jerusalem; (b) cleansing of the temple; (c) Thursday evening last supper; (d) Good Friday crucifixion; and (e) Easter morning resurrection. And what is most important to observe is that these events all happened at Jesus' own initiative and under his control (even the crucifixion he easily could have avoided at that time). In short, the sequence is one he *engineered,* not a series of things that *happened* to him. And our thesis is that this sequence can be understood as nothing other than a deliberate acting out (a living out) of the Zion Cycle.

The triumphal entry into Jerusalem (Zion) stands as a most appropriate opener to the sequence as a whole. It clearly is a symbolic, dramatic action intended to capture attention and make a statement. But stating what? Well, recall that Deutero's great Suffering-Servant oracle opened with what we called a theme-statement alerting readers to the meaning of the entire passage: "Behold, my servant shall prosper, he shall be lifted up, exalted to the heights." Jesus' action portrays something of the same paradox: The peaceable peasant preacher, leading a ragtag band of fishermen disciples, actually is (or is on the way to becoming) the conquering king of Zion. What this *entry* actually leads to is death on a cross—which in itself is a king's triumph. A *king* on a *donkey:* Isaiah's Messiah and Deutero's Suffering Servant are one and the same person.

The triumphal entry constitutes a fundamental reference to the Zion picture; and *Matthew's* interpretation of it best points us that way. Therein he quotes this prophecy:

Tell the daughter of Zion, "Here is your king, who comes to you in gentleness, riding on an ass, riding on the foal of a beast of burden."
Matthew 21:4-5.

The quotation is from Zechariah, a book we introduced earlier (see page 87 above). Recall that, although that book makes very great use of the Zion cycle, we found it to contain no hint of servanthood or vicarious suffering. In Zechariah, the quote Matthew uses reads:

Rejoice, rejoice, daughter of Zion, shout aloud, daughter of
Jerusalem; for see, your king is coming to you, *his cause won, his
victory gained,* humble and mounted on an ass, on a foal, the young
of a she-ass. He shall banish chariots from Ephraim and war-horses
from Jerusalem; the warrior's bow shall be banished. He shall speak
peaceably to every nation, and his rule shall extend from sea to sea.

Zechariah 9:9-10; italics mine.

In Zechariah's picture, it is clear that it is *after* he has won his
victory that the king rides to Zion on a donkey. This is a gesture of
true magnanimity and peace but nevertheless one with far different significance than when Matthew skips the italicized line of
the quotation and applies the shortened version to Jesus as he is
on his way to victory on a cross. Matthew's version brings in the
elements of "reverse fighting" and "exaltation through humiliation"; and thus the triumphal entry into Jerusalem takes on Suffering-Servant implications that Zechariah's original picture utterly lacked.

Following the triumphal entry, the various Gospels have
Jesus proceed directly to the cleansing of the temple, his condemning of its corruption and the chasing out of its money men
and their animals. However, more than any of the other writers,
Matthew again points us to an interpretation of the incident. All
that is required to bring the matter clear is to change the customary label from "the cleansing of the temple" to "the purgation
of Zion" and recall the words of Isaiah:

Once again I will act against you
to refine away your base metal as with potash
and purge all your impurities;
I will make your judges what once they were
and your counsellors like those of old. . . .
Justice shall redeem Zion.

Isaiah 1:25-27 (see page 74).

An even clearer precedent comes from Malachi, a book we
did not note earlier. It represents the late prophetic tradition and

focuses almost exclusively upon "the purgation of Zion" rather than upon the Zion cycle in its entirety—although there are clues to indicate that the writer was aware of the larger picture. But in any case, these are the words which surely must form the setting within which Jesus' action is to be understood:

> Look, I am sending my messenger who will clear a path before me. Suddenly the Lord whom you seek will come to his temple; the messenger of the covenant in whom you delight is here, here already, says Yahweh of Hosts. Who can endure the day of his coming? Who can stand firm when he appears? He is like a refiner's fire, like fuller's soap; he will take his seat, refining and purifying; he will purify the Levites and cleanse them like gold and silver, and so they shall be fit to bring offerings to Yahweh. Thus the offerings of Judah and Jerusalem shall be pleasing to Yahweh as they were in days of old, in years long past.
>
> Malachi 3:1-4.

Put it within the Zion framework and rename it "the purgation of Zion," and the cleansing of the temple becomes so "right" and so properly situated that it must be that Jesus himself was thinking in "Zion" terms. The purgation of Zion, which triggers Jesus' crucifixion, itself points to the stroke of the sword not of man which in its striking heals. What other alignment would make sense?

Matthew puts us on the track of this interpretation in a way that the other Gospels do not, because his account includes an element the others lack, namely, a description of Zion purged. The verses following the cleansing itself read:

> In the temple blind men and cripples came to him, and he healed them. The chief priests and doctors of the law saw the wonderful things he did, and heard the boys in the temple shouting, "Hosanna to the Son of David!"
>
> Matthew 21:14-15.

The Messiah (at least for the moment and in a symbolic way) has with justice redeemed Zion and restored her to what she was meant to be, a center of healing and servant ministry for the world.

Because the temple incident figures so large in current thought, we need to comment further. This event constitutes the golden text of the Bible for many modern pacifists; in fact, some of them give the impression that it is the only text they know. It forms the rationale for those who feel the need to become quite militant in their peacemaking. Aggressive confrontation is their style; and they claim to be following the temple-cleansing Jesus in applying something of his technique to the White House, Pentagon, and Selective Service offices.

But it won't wash; it won't even begin to wash! If what Jesus performed was the purgation of Zion, then it was not in any sense an act of human political activism. Its context is salvation history and not sociopolitical change. It is a peculiar work of *the Messiah,* a stroke of the sword not of man, precisely the sort of thing that Isaiah insisted human instrumentalities are not good enough to bring off. There is no suggestion at all that this is an aspect of his work in which Jesus called his disciples to share.

Besides, the action is directed toward *Zion,* not the world of the nations. When Jesus did encounter the world of the nations, namely, in his trial before Pilate, there was no attempt to confront, challenge, cleanse, or revolutionize. His attitude was, rather, "My kingdom is not of this world—i.e., what my kingship would require of you is so totally beyond your way of thinking that there is no sense even in trying to communicate it to you."

But if Christians are to find their place within the model of the cleansing of the temple, it is as *Zion* (= Israel = the new Israel). The passage calls them, then, to open themselves to purging by God so that, as delivered Zion, they are ready to perform a healing and foot-washing ministry to the world. Before long, we will come to Jesus' call to arms; but for sure, the cleansing of the temple isn't it! Yet, of course, we need to keep the other side of the coin in view, too: nation taking up sword against nation isn't Jesus' call either! Let us not be guilty of inviting pots to call the kettle black.

There is a further line of thought that relates to the purgation of Zion. In Matthew and some of the other accounts of Jesus' trial—and once, in Acts, clear down at the trial of Stephen—the charge is brought (and labeled by the Gospel writers as false) that Jesus had talked about how he would destroy the temple and build it again. The most likely explanation would seem to be that Jesus had spoken of the purgation of Zion and his words had been misunderstood and/or distorted. Recall that the Old Testament prophecies had varied between whether that purgation would represent devastation with a last minute reprieve or total destruction and a rebirth of Zion.

Finally, in Matthew 23, within Jesus' condemnation of the scribes and Pharisees, there is a passage that relates strongly to the purgation of Zion.

> O Jerusalem, Jerusalem, the city that murders the prophets and stones the messengers sent to her! How often have I longed to gather your children, as a hen gathers her brood under her wings; but you would not let me. Look, look! there is your temple, forsaken by God. And I tell you, you shall never see me until the time when you say, "Blessings on him who comes in the name of the Lord."
> Matthew 23:37-39.

This lament does not describe the entire action, of course. Nevertheless, we need always to remember that the New Testament understanding of peace goes deep enough that it can call for and include a painful and yet creative purgation of Zion, the holy community which itself will become, in turn, an instrument in the healing of the world. Truly Christian peacemakers must themselves be open to the purging of God.

The next item in the Holy Week sequence is the last supper. Its primary significance regarding the Zion cycle is as the occasion of the Servant Individual's incorporating into himself the Servant Israel (his community), making it his *body*, enlisting the group as fighters under his command, who are to go with him upon his way (the way of death and resurrection) to the winning of the peaceable kingdom of God. With the themes of "body," "covenant," "reverse fighting," "suffering servanthood," and "eschatological kingship," we already have seen that, in this instance, it is the Gospel of Luke (with a nice assist from John's footwashing) that does the best job of showing the Zion connections (see above, pp. 122-23).

The crucifixion itself next falls naturally into the sequence as the Suffering Servant's vicarious sacrifice—in quiet, defenseless love, his going to death. And as was noted earlier, that crucifixion could even be understood in terms of Isaiah's messianic Zion-tree being reduced to a stump. The Gospel accounts of the event include, at best, only vague overtones of this line of interpretation. However, we already have seen that the matter is made very explicit in Acts (see above, pp. 116 and 124-126) and we are about to see that it is also made so in Paul.

Finally, of course, the resurrection is of a piece with the foregoing—this as the Servant's vindication and victory beyond death, or as the green shoot growing out of the blasted stump. Here it is Luke's Gospel again that points the connection, this through the risen Jesus' own words to the disciples on the road to Emmaus (see above, p. 123). And Acts and the Epistles again are quite explicit.

But put these five events together as one sequence and—even without the Gospel writer's interpretive hints—it would still speak very strongly of the Old Testament Zion tradition. Rather evidently, the reason the writers' interpretations fit so well is that the sequence was done as Zion-fulfillment in the first place. There are no grounds for doubting that, with complete consciousness and clarity, Jesus of Nazareth took this Old Testament model as the call and program for his own career; his Holy Week scenario will support no other explanation. And it is just so fundamentally that our "peace argument" is built into the Christian gospel. There is no evading it!

The Pauline literature proves very important for our study, because Paul not only makes considerable use of the Zion tradition, he expands it in some very significant ways. For one thing, he breaks it free from any geographical and political limits regarding hereditary Israel and earthly Jerusalem—although not from its tie to the history of Jesus. He makes it universal and even cosmic in scope—although giving it very much of a present application at the same time. And finally, he gives a great deal of attention to the relationship between the Servant Individual (Jesus) and the Servant Israel (the Christian community).

At several points he, in effect, reiterates the entire cycle to demonstrate its range and breadth.

> The divine nature was his from the first; yet he did not think to snatch at equality with God, but made himself nothing, assuming the nature of a slave. Bearing the human likeness, revealed in human shape, he humbled himself, and in obedience accepted even death—death on a cross. Therefore God raised him to the heights and bestowed on him the name above all names, that at the name of Jesus every knee should bow—in heaven, on earth, and in the depths—and every tongue confess, "Jesus Christ is Lord," to the glory of God the Father.
>
> Philippians 2:6-11.

> Through him God chose to reconcile the whole universe to himself, making peace through the shedding of his blood upon the cross—to reconcile all things, whether on earth or in heaven, through him alone.
>
> Colossians 1:20.

The way is that of a servant—even "slave"—humiliated in his suffering and defenselessness to the extent of death, death on a cross. But then he is raised and exalted by God to win the attention and loyalty of all and so create peace, a peace that reconciles all things in heaven and on earth. The Zion picture has been stretched as far as there is to go—and its "peace" also (the reconciliation of *all things*).

Yet, in another passage, the apostle does manage to go a step further (or perhaps *two* steps further):

> One man died for all and therefore all mankind has died. His pur-

pose in dying for all was that men, while still in life, should cease to live for themselves, and should live for him who for their sake died and was raised to life. . . . When anyone is united to Christ, there is a new world; the old order has gone, and a new order has already begun. From first to last this has been the work of God. He has reconciled us men to himself through Christ, and he has enlisted us in this service of reconciliation.

2 Corinthians 5:14-18.

It is obvious—so *very* obvious, so *painfully* obvious—that Paul's time of perfect peace, the reconciliation of all things, is not yet. But this does not indicate by any means that we still are back with the Old Testament prophets who, at best, could express only the hope of what God *would* do someday. No, Paul tells us that when anyone is united to Christ, the new order already has begun. The world's peace is not completed, but it is in progress—and even now *we* can be a part of it.

This is not to suggest that Christians now have the wherewithal to rush out and set the world right. No, from first to last it is *God's* work, the apostle says. Nevertheless, he now enlists us into this great work of universal reconciliation. *What* that means, we will discover a bit later.

However, one thing is clear even at this point: the aim of the gospel is not simply peace for the individual heart, oblivious to the state of society and the world. It may *begin* with inner peace for the individual, it certainly *involves* peace for the individual, it may work *through* the peace of the individual; but its goal is the peace of the world, and it is at this very moment making progress toward that goal.

The goal of world peace has not yet been reached, but the *victory* that guarantees it is described in the *past* tense:

For he has forgiven us all our sins; he has cancelled the bond which pledged us to the decrees of the law. It stood against us, but he has set it aside, nailing it to the cross. On that cross he despoiled the cosmic powers and authorities, and boldly made spectacle of them, leading them as captives in his triumphal procession.

Colossians 2:13-15.

That, my friends, is pretty strong Holy War talk—and it answers a number of the questions raised by the Holy War talk we have encountered up to this point. Man, Genesis told us, did and does tell God to get out of the way and preferably to wander off and drop dead. This created and does create something of a strained relationship which, accordingly, moves God to fight. He doesn't have to take that lying down! But the motive of God's fight, Paul now tells us, is not to "do man in" but to convince him that the enormity of that insult to God can be and has been forgiven, that the two now can be reconciled. And this victory, we are told, was won at Skull Hill.

However, the real enemy, the one God truly is determined to do in, is what Paul calls "the cosmic powers and authorities." These are not human beings but precisely the *in*humanities that infest the race and lead men to rebel against God and their fellows. These dark menaces are not easy to track down and identify; it is certain they are bigger, more invisible, and harder to handle than is indicated by the diagnoses of our psychologists, sociologists, and politicians. Yet, although hard to pinpoint, we feel their haunt in our personal lives and see their all-too-palpable tracks in the wreckage of the world around us. But even these, the apostle insists, got bested at Skull Hill; and although they aren't completely off the scene yet, they are being led by the nose in the Messiah's triumphal procession. Paul knows about a Holy War that makes the earlier ones look like innocent children's pillow fights.

But of course, Joshua didn't know (couldn't know) all that Paul knows—which is why he could do only the best that he did know and go with human arms against human enemies. It was Jesus who got things straightened out so that Paul could explain them to us.

Paul knows, too, that it is through "reverse fighting" that this war is won. And the strategies are figured according to the wisdom of God and not the customary wisdom of Nimrodian apple-calculation:

And yet I do speak words of wisdom to those who are ripe for it, not a wisdom belonging to this passing age, nor to any of its governing powers, which are declining to their end; I speak God's hidden wisdom, his secret purpose framed from the very beginning to bring us to our full glory.

1 Corinthians 2:6-7.

And in his wisdom, God chose to win the victory through means that are most characteristic of the Suffering Servant:

Yet, to shame the wise, God has chosen what the world counts folly, and to shame what is strong, God has chosen what the world counts weakness. He has chosen things low and contemptible, mere nothings, to overthrow the existing order.

1 Corinthians 1:27-28.

However, if the battle is fought by means of weakness and defenselessness, then plainly the victory comes not as an inherent consequence of the means used but through the resurrection power of the God who raises the Servant:

How vast [are] the resources of power open to us who trust in him. They are measured by his strength and the might which he exerted in Christ when he raised him from the dead, when he enthroned him at his right hand in the heavenly realms, far above all government and authority, all power and dominion, and any title of sovereignty that can be named, not only in this age but in the age to come.

Ephesians 1:19-21.

This is the *quality* of resurrection power; in another passage Paul describes *how* that power will be used:

As in Adam all men die, so in Christ all will be brought to life; but each in his own proper place: Christ the firstfruits, and afterwards, at his coming, those who belong to Christ. Then comes the end, when he delivers up the kingdom to God the Father, after abolishing every kind of domination, authority, and power. For he is destined to reign until God has put all enemies under his feet; and the last enemy to be abolished is death.

1 Corinthians 15:22-26.

Both of these passages make it clear that resurrection is the key not only to the Messiah's personal experience of victory but also to the cosmic transformation of the whole. Further, resurrection is not merely the hope for an individual believer's survival after death; it is the hope of a new world order gained through the defeat of the dominations, authorities, and powers—the real enemies of God.

The goal and outcome of this work is a peace of such quality and magnitude as neither the Old Testament Zion prophets nor the contemporary peace movement has dared to dream.

> For *the created universe* waits with eager expectation for God's sons to be revealed.... *The universe itself* is to be freed from the shackles of mortality and enter upon the liberty and splendor of the children of God.
>
> Romans 8:19, 21; italics mine.

Sometimes Paul can describe even this peace in rather strong Holy War language: "The God of *peace* will soon crush Satan beneath your feet" (Romans 16:20). But what he actually is talking about is an incredible quality of *reconciliation*. What he says in the following about the Jew-Gentile cleft he undoubtedly would be ready to say regarding all the severances that make ours a shattered globe.

> For he is himself our peace. Gentiles and Jews, he has made the two one, and in his own body of flesh and blood has broken down the enmity which stood like a dividing wall between them; for he annulled the law with its rules and regulations, so as to create out of the two a single new humanity in himself, thereby making peace. This was his purpose, to reconcile the two in a single body to God through the cross, on which he killed the enmity. So he came and proclaimed the good news: peace to you who were far off, and peace to those who were near by; for through him we both alike have access to the Father in the one Spirit.
>
> Ephesians 2:14-18.

Peace, it should be abundantly clear by now, is not simply

one of the ethical counsels which Jesus maybe did and maybe did
not teach; it is a central focus and goal of the gospel. However, it
does not follow that anyone who makes peace a central passion of
his life, regardless of how he defines it or goes after it, is by that
token a Christian; the gospel is as strong on some of the "whats"
and "hows" of peace as it is on the fact that peace is the goal.

Also, as we mentioned, Paul has made it abundantly clear
that Christian peace does not refer merely to a desirable inner
state of the individual. Christian peace can include that—and
most assuredly does—but it also has to do with the breaking down
of societal dividing walls and the creation of a single new humanity, something that must involve outward as well as inward
arrangements of peace.

But what Paul does next—and this is his special contribution—is to explore and elucidate the relationship between the
Servant Individual and the Servant Israel. And this, of course, is to
start us on the crucial question: "How do *we* fit in?" In some
respects Paul might seem to be going beyond the Zion tradition;
but it also is possible to understand him as expanding and filling
in the basic concepts found in Deutero-Isaiah.

> For in baptism you were buried with him, in baptism also you were
> raised to life with him through your faith in the active power of God
> who raised him from the dead.
>
> Colossians 2:12.

> For if we have become incorporate with him in a death like his, we
> shall also be one with him in a resurrection like his. . . . For in dying
> as he died, he died to sin, once for all, and in living as he lives, he
> lives to God. In the same way you must regard yourselves as dead to
> sin and alive to God, in union with Christ Jesus.
>
> Romans 6:5, 10-11.

Deutero, we saw, gave us such a blurred distinction between
the Servant Individual and the Servant Israel that the two tended
to merge. Paul accomplishes something of the same sort—except
not simply by blurring them. Now the Servant Israel (i.e., the

Christian believer in his faith community), by giving himself completely to the lordship of the Servant Individual and by identifying completely with him, becomes in effect "incorporate" or "in union" with him. Elsewhere Paul describes the same movement as the community's becoming "the body of Christ."

But this incorporation is so complete, the apostle tells us, that the believer reiterates in his own experience the death-and-resurrection experience of the Servant himself ("buried *with him*" and "raised to life *with him*" through the same power that accomplished it for him). It is this death-and-resurrection recapitulation that baptism portrays.

What baptism particularly signifies is an *inner* experience of dying to sin and being raised "so also we might set our feet upon the new path of life" (Romans 6:4). But as we follow Paul further we shall discover that by no means does he *limit* this recapitulation to the realm of inward experience; the outward history of the Servant Individual also, in a very real way, is to become the history of Servant Israel.

Yet, although the "incorporation" is meant to be just this complete, Paul never confuses Servant Israel with the Servant Individual—any more than Deutero did. They have some distinctions of role and function that are absolute. For instance, Servant Israel is called to undergo purgation and live as the true Zion; but he is not invited to be the Purger either of Zion or the world. He is called defenselessly to suffer as does the Servant Individual; but nowhere is it claimed that his sufferings atone for the sins of the world. For Christians to claim that the world is healed through *our* scourgings or that the Lord has laid upon *us* the guilt of mankind would be sacrilege. The Christian's suffering *witnesses to* that of the Servant but certainly does not substitute for or assume the significance of his. And finally, although Servant Israel is to be resurrected in victory, his resurrection in no wise represents an exaltation to the status of "lord." Servant Israel does become incorporate with Servant Individual and reiterates his history but nevertheless remains subordinate to and dependent upon him.

Not infrequently Paul presents himself to his Christian brethren as something of a specimen of what they should become. In so doing, he portrays himself after the likeness of a suffering servant. The matter cannot be sheer coincidence. Paul knows that the way of the church (and the Christian) is to be that of her Lord. He can put it in a sentence: "I have made myself every man's servant, to win over as many as possible" (1 Corinthians 9:19). He can elucidate the matter at length, pushing the contrast between himself and the "sensible" Christians who operate according to the world's wisdom:

> It seems to me that God has made us apostles the most abject of mankind. We are like men condemned to death in the arena, a spectacle to the whole universe—angels as well as men. We are fools for Christ's sake, while you are such sensible Christians. We are weak; you are so powerful. We are in disgrace; you are honored. To this day we go hungry and thirsty and in rags; we are roughly handled; we wander from place to place; we wear ourselves out working with our own hands. They curse us, and we bless; they persecute us, and we submit to it; they slander us, and we humbly make our appeal. We are treated as the scum of the earth, the dregs of humanity, to this very day.
>
> 1 Corinthians 4:9-13.

The picture cannot help but call to mind not only Deutero's description of the Suffering Servant but the history of Jesus as well. Also, it is certainly the direct opposite of Nimrodian warmaking—being, rather, the portrayal of a defenseless and nonresisting vulnerability that does not raise a voice in the streets and like a sheep before its shearers is dumb. One of the concluding phrases, "we humbly make our appeal," even should make some of our modern protesters stop and think.

In another passage, Paul reveals the significance that his suffering carries:

> Hard-pressed on every side, we are never hemmed in; . . . struck down, we are not left to die. Wherever we go we carry death with us

in our body, the death that Jesus died, that in this body also life may reveal itself, the life that Jesus lives.

2 Corinthians 4:8-10.

Clearly, his suffering (and his rising above suffering) represent a reiteration of Jesus'. However, in no sense is it to be understood as a *duplication of* Jesus but only a *witness to* him. Those who see Paul are to see Jesus' death and resurrection and not Paul's own.

Finally, in this connection, the apostle explains that he *can* dare and endure the suffering of a servant only because he has the support of the Christ with whom he is incorporate. A personal affliction is his example, although surely he means to be speaking in terms of general principle as well:

> Three times I begged the Lord to rid me of it, but his answer was: "My grace is all you need; power comes to its full strength in weakness." I shall therefore prefer to find my joy and pride in the very things that are my weakness; and then the power of Christ will come and rest upon me. Hence I am well content, for Christ's sake, with weakness, contempt, persecution, hardship, and frustration; for when I am weak, then I am strong.
>
> 2 Corinthians 12:8-10.

The clear implication is that the power of Christ is available only when one is in union with him and meeting life in his way, namely, in the weakness of a servant.

And then, speaking not particularly of his own suffering but of that of the servant community, Paul affirms that, through "reverse fighting," the way of the Servant leads to life and victory both for the Servant himself and for those incorporate in him: "True, he died on a cross in weakness, but he lives by the power of God; and we who share his weakness shall by the power of God live with him in your service" (2 Corinthians 13:4).

It might seem that we have come a long way from Holy War—talking now about vulnerability, death, and weakness. Yes, but also No. For out of the same literature and without any contradiction at all comes a passage such as this:

Finally then, find your strength in the Lord, in his mighty power. Put on all the armor which God provides, so that you may be able to stand firm against the devices of the devil. For our fight is not against human foes, but against cosmic powers, against the authorities and potentates of this dark world, against the superhuman forces of evil in the heavens. Therefore, take up God's armor; then you will be able to stand your ground when things are at their worst, to complete every task and still to stand.

Ephesians 6:10-13.

In the catalog of arms that follows these verses, a couple of the items are identical with the armor that the third part of Isaiah, in one of the most warlike passages we have quoted, describes God himself as wearing (see page 110 above). The line of development we have traced in getting to this point is straight and logical.

There is an important point to note in the passage above; the entire description is *defensive* in character. The instructions are to "stand your ground," not go out to conquer the world, turn it around, or force it to lay down its arms and be peaceful. Yet "reverse fighting" is a true fighting that will require real strength and bravery and endurance. The Christian will need all the armor that God provides. And of course, the ultimate in such armor is the power of *resurrection*. He who has this can risk death—and even *take* death—and still never be wiped out; for God, in his love, is there to set him back up. Paul knew all about it:

"We are being done to death for thy sake all day long," as Scripture says; "we have been treated like sheep for slaughter"—and yet, in spite of all, overwhelming victory is ours through him who loved us. For I am convinced that there is nothing in death or life, in the realm of spirits or superhuman powers, in the world as it is or the world as it shall be, in the forces of the universe, in heights or depths—nothing in all creation that can separate us from the love of God in Christ Jesus our Lord.

Romans 8:36-39.

6

To Whom It May Concern, Greetings . . . Signed: The King

Anyone who wishes to be a follower of mine must leave self behind; he must take up his cross, and come with me. Whoever cares for his own safety is lost; but if a man will let himself be lost for my sake and for the gospel, that man is safe.

—King Jesus (Mark 8:34-35)

Strictly speaking, I suppose, it is only now that our book becomes King Jesus' instructions to *us*. Nevertheless, the preceding five chapters have been proper and even necessary in establishing who is this King Jesus, for what end he fights, who is the enemy he confronts, by what authority he enlists an army, what are the terms of his draft, and what are the veterans' benefits. That done, his explicit training drills and lectures will make much better sense and can be gone through in rather short order.

Indeed, the question that here engages us is: Are Jesus' own teachings appropriate to our picture of a Servant-Messiah instructing those who would fight under his command and after his example? To get the answer it will not be necessary to gather each and every verse that might have implications regarding peace and war. The best book taking this approach is probably G. H. C. Macgregor's *New Testament Basis of Pacifism* or John Ferguson's

The Politics of Love. Our interest is only in locating the major thrust of Jesus' teaching and determining how it fits in with the pattern we have been developing up to this point.

Perhaps the best way of getting at that major thrust is to start with the most compact statement possible and then follow out its implications and enlargements. Put most briefly, Jesus' teachings can be reduced to a two-word sentence which isn't even a teaching; it's a command: "Follow me!" I don't know how many times those words or variations of them appear in the Gospels, but that isn't important. There is not the slightest doubt but that Jesus' teaching starts here, centers here, ends here, and rests here.

Jesus never was and never hinted at being a philosopher or teacher of ethics who let fall pearls of wisdom about how good people should live and who then passed on, leaving the good people to decide for themselves how great the teachings actually are and to what extent they ought to be observed. Not for one moment! What we meet in this Jesus is a *king*—at least enough of a king to take it upon himself to institute a draft, put the bee on people, and enlist them into his service. "Follow me!"

The Holy War pattern applies this far even if no farther. The old Selective Service System of Yahweh has come back into effect. And in this case the king isn't like a United States President who says, "Now you people go on out there and fight; and you can be sure that I'm always right back here in the White House (or my bomb shelter) urging you on!" No, this king—like Yahweh of old—leads the fight from out front. "Follow me! And you'd better hurry up or I'll have it all done before you get in on it—and then won't you feel left out!"

And again as with Yahweh of old, "Follow me" means "Fight *as* I fight; a ballerina stance is the only proper one." And when the king is this one, that obviously will have to entail a career of humble service to one's fellowmen; a readiness in every situation to accept suffering rather than inflict it on another; willingness to risk defeat and even death in the faith that, if needs be, God can pull off a resurrection to put things right. "Follow me!"

Finally, let it be said that every bit of teaching and counsel given by Jesus comes out of this "follow me" context and cannot be understood apart from it. There is here no general teaching, no humane wisdom, no universal guidance that anyone might decide to practice for himself with some assurance that it will pay off in success and happiness. No, if they are to be workable at all, every teaching of Jesus must assume the relationship of discipleship and must, in fact, *require* that relationship with its enablements of being "incorporate with Christ" and the possibility of resurrection. "Follow me!"

What all this means, then, is that the material of our previous chapter now has jumped over into this one. *Who* Jesus is and *what* was his history is part of his *teaching*—perhaps an even more important part than his sayings. Such necessarily is the case when the sum of that teaching is: "King Jesus wants *you*. Follow me!"

Our headnote from Mark 8 starts us upon an exploration of what it means to "follow me" and indicates that we are on the right track. Here is a very basic statement regarding "reverse fighting." Wars and fightings, we discovered clear back in Genesis, arise largely out of man's attempt to construct *security* for himself; and Jesus says explicitly, "Whoever cares for his own safety is lost." His way is the absolute reverse of the world's way. And note, too, that if there is to be any sense at all in the thought, "If a man will let himself be lost, that man is safe," it has to assume the intervention of an outside power through something like a resurrection; "letting oneself be lost" cannot naturally and of itself be equated with "becoming safe."

Elsewhere from Mark comes another key link in the "follow me" chain:

> You know that in the world the recognized rulers lord it over their subjects, and their great men make them feel the weight of authority. That is not the way with you; among you, whoever wants to be great must be your servant, and whoever wants to be first must be willing to be slave of all. For even the Son of Man did not come

to be served but to serve, and to give up his life as a ransom for
many.
Mark 10:42-45.

Here again it is made plain that Jesus is himself the model of
what he teaches and that the command, therefore, is properly,
"Follow me!" But in this case we are taken beyond simply "letting oneself be lost" and directed to "*give yourself* in humble
service"—a slightly different idea but still one that is a complete
reversal of the world's way of wars and fightings. In the two-word
term, "Suffering Servant," both factors call for equal emphasis: he
both *serves* and *suffers;* his service leads to suffering, and his suffering is itself the greatest service he performs.

The specific teachings and instructions of Jesus fit beautifully
within the framework we have developed. To get at them, we
propose to go to only two major passages from the Gospel of Matthew: the Sermon on the Mount and the commissioning of the
disciples to their ministry in the world. Of course, more material
could be found elsewhere; but Matthew is the greatest presenter
of the teachings of Jesus, and what he gives us will more than suf-
fice.

First, then, the Sermon on the Mount. Has anyone ever
considered that the Beatitudes describe a suffering servant?

> How blest are those who know their need of God;
> . . .[who] are sorrowful;
> . . .[who are] of a gentle spirit;
> . . .who hunger and thirst to see right prevail;
> . . .who show mercy;
> . . .whose hearts are pure;
> . . .[who] are peacemakers;
> . . .who have suffered persecution for the cause of right.
Matthew 5:3-10.

You have learned that our forefathers were told, "Do not commit
murder; anyone who commits murder must be brought to judgment." But what I tell you is this: Anyone who nurses anger against
his brother must be brought to judgment. If he abuses his brother

he must answer for it to the court; if he sneers at him he will have to answer for it in the fires of hell.

Matthew 5:21-22.

You have learned that they were told, "Eye for eye, tooth for tooth." But what I tell you is this: "Do not set yourself against the man who wrongs you. If someone slaps you on the right cheek, turn and offer him your left. If a man wants to sue you for your shirt, let him have your coat as well. If a man in authority makes you go one mile, go with him two. Give when you are asked to give; and do not turn your back on a man who wants to borrow. You have learned that they were told, "Love your neighbor, hate your enemy." But what I tell you is this: Love your enemies and pray for your persecutors. . . . There must be no limit to your goodness, as your heavenly Father's goodness knows no bounds.

Matthew 5:38-44, 48.

If you forgive others the wrongs they have done, your heavenly Father will also forgive you; but if you do not forgive others, then the wrongs you have done will not be forgiven by your Father.

Matthew 6:14-15.

Pass no judgment, and you will not be judged. For as you judge others, so you will yourselves be judged, and whatever measure you deal to others will be dealt back to you. Why do you look at the speck of sawdust in your brother's eye, with never a thought for the great plank in your own?

Matthew 7:1-3.

Always treat others as you would like them to treat you: that is the Law and the prophets.

Matthew 7:12.

Not everyone who calls me "Lord, Lord" will enter the kingdom of Heaven, but only those who do the will of my heavenly Father.

Matthew 7:21.

Such teachings, which could be multiplied at length, are so clear and uncomplicated that they require no commentary at all. But can they be understood as anything other than the Suffering-Servant Messiah calling draftees to follow him?

The tenth chapter of Matthew presents Jesus giving specific instructions as to how his disciples are to conduct themselves. If anything, Suffering-Servant themes and echoes of the larger Zion tradition come through even stronger here than in the Sermon on the Mount.

> So Jesus went round all the towns and villages teaching in their synagogues, announcing the good news of the Kingdom, and curing every kind of ailment and disease. The sight of the people moved him to pity: they were like sheep without a shepherd, harassed and helpless; and he said to his disciples, "The crop is heavy, but laborers are scarce; you must therefore beg the owner to send laborers to harvest his crop." Then he called his twelve disciples to him and gave them authority to cast out unclean spirits and to cure every kind of ailment and disease.... "As you go proclaim the message: 'The kingdom of Heaven is upon you.' Heal the sick, raise the dead, cleanse lepers, cast out devils. You received without cost; give without charge."
>
> Matthew 9:35—10:1, 7-8.

The connection could not be made more plain. The Servant Individual has dedicated himself totally to serving the needs of men and seeking their highest welfare; and he commissions Servant Israel to engage in the same ministry. This is a major aspect of his fight against the powers and authorities which are the enemy of mankind.

> Look, I send you out like sheep among wolves; be wary as serpents, innocent as doves. And be on your guard, for men will hand you over to their courts, they will flog you in the synagogues, and you will be brought before governors and kings, for my sake.... All will hate you for your allegiance to me.... The pupil should be content to share his teacher's lot, the servant to share his master's.... So do not be afraid of them.
>
> Matthew 10:16-18, 22, 25-26.

Through their service, the followers of Jesus will come into conflict with society—into conflict with the state and the powerful of the world, even with members of their own families. Suffering will be theirs. (It is, by the way, some of this material that *Luke* uses in describing the end of the age [see page 122 above].) However, in all this, they simply are sharing the lot of their leader and king. But even as he did, they are to meet the situation as defenseless sheep and innocent doves rather than assuming the character of the wolves of the world. This, too, is an aspect of their fight against the powers.

> Do not fear those who kill the body, but cannot kill the soul. Fear him rather who is able to destroy both soul and body in hell. Are not sparrows two a penny? Yet without your Father's leave not one of them can fall to the ground. As for you, even the hairs of your head have all been counted. So have no fear; you are worth more than any number of sparrows.
>
> Matthew 10:28-31.

How can these disciples afford to suffer in complete defense-lessness and yet have no fear regarding either their own survival or the success of their cause? Because they know that their fight is *God's* fight—that he can and will take care both of them and the cause, even in death and beyond, even if resurrection should be required. The thought is little different from what we found in the original Holy War tradition.

However, note well, the text definitely does *not* say: "Have no fear; your selfless works, noble intentions, and beautiful expressions of love will win over your opponents and make them as nice as you are. Thus you and your cause will be saved." Anyone who presumes to adopt defenselessness for himself, without regard to King Jesus, or becoming incorporate with him, or sharing his resurrection—he would be better off if he had a lit-tle more fear than he does.

> You must not think that I have come to bring peace to the earth; I have not come to bring peace, but a sword. I have come to set a man against his father, a daughter against her mother, a son's wife against her mother-in-law; and a man will find his enemies under his own roof. No man is worthy of me who cares more for father or

mother than for me; no man is worthy of me who does not take up
his cross and walk in my footsteps. By gaining his life a man will lose
it; by losing his life for my sake, he will gain it.
Matthew 10:34-39.

The way of the servant—both that of Servant Individual and
Servant Israel—may be that of loving service and defenseless suffering; it most assuredly is. Its methods may be the very opposite
of what the world calls "fighting"; they most assuredly are. But it
is *war* nonetheless; and King Jesus is willing to call it that—in the
unmistakable language of Holy War. To fight with him, to fight
in his way, calls for all the strength, courage, endurance, risk-tak-
ing, brains, guts, sweat, and blood that any other war requires.
The case is simply that these things are applied differently: to taking up a cross, following in the footsteps of the Servant-Messiah,
losing one's life in order to gain it. King Jesus—like Yahweh of
old—is a man of war; and his call, like Yahweh's, is "follow me!"

The teachings of Jesus were never intended to stand on their
own two feet as independent, self-evident truth—particularly regarding the matter of defenselessness. However, in their proper
setting, as King Jesus' command for his enlisted men to follow
him, they are found to fit perfectly the pattern we have been trac-
ing through the Bible. In fact, once we have come at the matter
so, it is well-nigh inconceivable how Christians could read their
Bibles and find it permitting (let alone *approving*) their participation in the wars and fightings of the world. Yet a great majority of
Christians have read their Bibles without feeling a problem at all.
How have they managed it?

Well, for one thing, if a person is so inclined, he can locate
scattered verses and can manipulate the interpretation of some
others to point to (or at least open the possibility of) a conclusion
different from ours. However, in so doing, he has to ignore and
blind himself to the major thrust we have traced. It is a case, I
guess, of what we all are prone to—that is, *making* scripture say
what we think it *should* say. But we shall not spend our time try-

ing to rebut these otherwise-pointing verses and interpretations; if the positive witness of the major thrust won't convince, nothing will.

However, most Christian supporters of war would not dispute our interpretation of the teachings of Jesus; those are all too clear. But they would question our *application* of them. They point out that, all the way through, Jesus speaks in terms of person-to-person actions, how the Christian individual is to conduct himself toward the other individuals with whom he comes into personal contact. He nowhere suggests that the same methods should regulate national policy, societal activity, the life of institutions, or even the life of the individual when he is acting as the representative of government or is in the role of political or social functionary.

The observation is correct; but it may be the case (and I believe it is) that Jesus refuses to admit that a Christian ever *can* disown the personal responsibility of his having been drafted into the forces of the Servant-Messiah. That call takes precedence over any and all others; and thus, any social role which would require the Christian to act to the contrary is, by that very token, prohibited. "No man can serve two masters; choose, then, whom you will serve." And so Jesus *needs* to speak only in terms of person-to-person action, because he intends that such considerations govern the behavior of the Christian in whatever setting he finds himself.

On the other hand, if Jesus did not intend the suffering-servant approach to apply in all cases, then there is a very serious defect in the Christian gospel—and we ought to be honest enough to come right out and say so. For if the suffering-servant ethic is not meant to apply in societal situations, then the gospel gives *not the slightest hint* as to what ethic is to apply; there is no other ethic in the New Testament. And we have been given a very inadequate gospel indeed if it gives no help or guidance regarding major sectors of people's life together.

But our knowledge of the Zion tradition makes this proposal

preposterous in any case. Jesus' teachings are part and parcel of that Zion tradition and are to be understood as such. That tradition—from its very beginnings in the theory of Holy War through its culmination in the Servant-Messiah of the cross and resurrection—speaks in terms of world historical agents and points toward the goal of political, societal peace among the nations. Its methods are not those of the world, but its action is in the world and it is purposed for the sake of the world. Everything about the Zion tradition resists the attempt to internalize it into merely inner, spiritual experience or to confine it to the level of merely one-to-one, personal relationships. It is God's economy and fight for the world; and its ethic is God's way of peace for the nations. As far as the Bible is concerned, it is the suffering-servant ethic or none at all.

"But, then, why don't Christians see it that way, accept it and follow it?"

They are afraid it won't work. On the personal level, where it is possible to operate in terms of a one-to-one relationship, they can see how it *might* work—at least in many situations. If I am willing to perform deeds of loving service for my nasty neighbor and not strike back when he gets mean, I just may be able to win him over and save the day. And even if I fail, the loss wouldn't be too great; the worst he would do is to chuck a rock through my picture window. Sure, I'm willing to give it a go and at least *try* Jesus' way.

But if you are talking about Russian Communists lobbing nuclear warheads at our cities, there isn't a chance in the world that Christian love and defenselessness would stop them. And in this case, if our suffering-servanthood failed, the loss would not be merely a picture window; our picture, the whole picture of America, would go out for good. You *can't* take Jesus' way in a situation like that; it won't work.

Personally, I much prefer such an argument to the one which says, "Oh, but the way of love *will* work—even in the kind of situation you describe. If only we let the Communists know that we *really* love them. All we have to do is make love, not war. Give *peace* a chance . . . and it will win its own way!"

Both those who think that "peace" will work and those who think it won't are dead wrong (*dead* wrong). For both overlook the fact that neither Jesus nor any of the Zion writers ever suggested that the way of the suffering servant would "work" or even was supposed to work. After all, beyond dispute, Jesus was the greatest practitioner of the way who ever lived. And where did it get him? He couldn't make it work (if that is what he was trying to do) even on the person-to-person level. His enemies rolled right over his defenseless love as if it weren't even there, did to him as they pleased, and hung him up to die. He lost both his life *and* his cause; his followers betrayed, denied, and deserted him; and had it not been for a totally separate and independent act of God, Christianity would have become a dead issue right then and there. So if it was Jesus' intention to teach nonviolent, suffering love as a sociopolitical technique for the furthering of good causes, his own example surely isn't much of a recommendation.

This is not to say that defenselessness *never* wins over an enemy or brings its cause to accomplishment; there have been examples where circumstances were such that the way of love did work—in some cases quite dramatically and some of these cases quite recently. Nevertheless, *as a self-operative technique*, the way of love is very unreliable at best and completely ineffectual in many situations. Not that *violence* has a better record; it stands even less chance of proving useful in the promotion of good causes. Our critique of nonviolence is in no sense a recommendation for violence.

But if defenselessness is being used simply as a *technique*, then, as soon as it becomes apparent that it is not going to work, one has the right—and indeed, the *responsibility*—to abandon it and try something else. The sole proof of a technique and its only reason for being is that it will "work."

And yet Jesus' command and example make it plain that defenseless love is the order of the day whether it gives any evidence of working or not, even when it becomes obvious that it is leading to nothing but death on a cross. Why? Because the servant is not a societal engineer trying a recommended procedure; he is an enlisted man obeying the orders of his king. It is not his technique that is being tested but his trust and loyalty. And if the technique fails and the servant's way goes to defeat and death, that is not the end of the story; for the power of victory never did seat in the efficacy of the technique but in the will of the God who ordered the venture in the first place and who has promised to do whatever is necessary to bring the matter through to success, even if that necessity should entail a resurrection.

All this means that the Christian servant needs *first* to give attention to the quality of his *faith* rather than his *love*. Mere human love has not the power to quell our wars and fightings in any case; the lovers themselves have too much of Cain and Nimrod in them to be able to turn humanity around. Only resurrection power can do it; and only faith in the possibility of resurrection can steel the servant to love his way to the cross—and beyond. *His* love, then, becomes an expression of *that* faith; and this is the faith and love God can use as the hope of the world. The easy, idealistic slogans urging all of us simply to quit being fighters and start being lovers just aren't with it; the servant is called to demonstrate a *particular* quality of love that comes only as the expression of a *particular* resurrection faith that depends upon the power of a *particular* God.

Ultimately, then, the Christian failure to follow the way of the Suffering Servant in all situations must be seen as a failure of faith in God's ability to resurrect and his promise that he *will* resurrect not only individuals but also his Zion community and his world. Many Christians, I am confident, would be willing to take the servant's risk simply on an individual basis. They *would* defenselessly lay down their own lives by way of faith acting through love. God, they are convinced, can and will take care of them. But when more people are involved—their loved ones, their compatriots, or the nation itself—then apparently they become doubtful that God and his reverse methods of fighting are adequate for the situation. Love *as a technique* will not work, and a resurrection promise is too "iffy"; so the suffering-servant role is jettisoned in favor of something nearer to what this world calls fighting.

It is strange. Most Christians would be quick to believe that Isaiah was correct in counseling his non-Christian brethren to trust Yahweh to deliver Zion from the Assyrians; yet we didn't believe that the God who resurrected Jesus Christ was capable of delivering us from a Hitler. At that point, we thought, the God of the Suffering Servant desired that we resort to arms.

We are willing to risk our personal lives for the faith, but we aren't willing to risk the life of the nation. But if God can resurrect the one, he can resurrect the other—that is, if the survival of the United States of America is a contributive factor in his plan for mankind. And the Bible nowhere suggests that the way of the Suffering Servant is meant to apply only at times, in certain limited situations where *we can see* the possibility of its being successful; that thought stems from our desire to be *like God*, possess a self-sufficient knowledge in ourselves, and control the means of our own security. But quite the contrary, within its context of the Zion tradition, the way of the Servant is given the broadest possible application; it is presented as God's intended means of establishing peace and justice for the world and reconciling all things to himself.

Also, it must be pointed out that this indictment for faith-failure must be served against almost as many of our Christian peace advocates as our Christian warriors. Listening to what the peace people say, watching what they do, and reading their literature would indicate that, in general, their faith centers in the potential of a human (apple-inspired) societal technique rather than in a God of demonstrated resurrection capability. This being the case, the all-too-likely outcome is that, when the world refuses to respond to this technique as he thinks it should, the peace-maker either becomes despondent and drops his efforts or be-

comes desperate and begins to bend those efforts in the direction
of violence, near violence, and political machination. However,
neither armed warfare nor man's go-it-alone efforts at peacemaking will qualify as service under King Jesus—even though, undoubtedly, any sort of peacemaking should be accepted as
preferable to war-making.

We have insisted that the suffering-servant approach is not a
self-contained technique that can be counted upon to "work" in
and of itself. Yet when it has the help of God, is supplemented
and used by him for his ends and purposes, the biblical picture
certainly is that ultimately it works—and that ultimately it is the
only thing that *will* work. Can we say anything, then, about *how*
it works? Well, we can try.

It is easy to figure out how *wars and fightings* work, how
their evil conducts itself. The key concept, as we saw back in
Genesis, is "escalation"—or perhaps even closer to the mark,
"chain reaction."

Warrior I gets it in for Person II and lets him have it. This
tends to make Person II unhappy, so he strikes back and thus becomes Warrior II. As Warriors I and II are going at it, Person III
steps in to try and stop them. But in the process, he gets punched,
punches back, and becomes Warrior III. Person IV comes to the
defense of Warrior I and so is credentialed as Warrior IV. Before
you know it, Person MDCLXVI's flower bed gets run over by a
tank, and he runs down to enlist as Warrior MDCLXVI. It soon
becomes obvious that we should have started out with something
other than Roman numerals if we ever hoped to make our point,
but perhaps it is made in any case. Evil is going great guns (I almost wrote "growing by leaps and bounds," but "going great
guns" is so much more appropriate). Violence by nature is so
constituted that its very existence insures its spreading; it matures
at a 100 percent rate of interest compounded as often as new vic-
tims get sucked in.

The human impulse for stopping such maniac progression is

to jump in with enough clout to put down all the previously assembled clouters. But more times than not, *that* clout simply makes all the clouters more cloutish and brings even more and bigger clouters onto the scene as well. And even if one party does amass enough clout to do the job, the end result is not peace but merely repressed hostility. Using Violence II to stop Violence I automatically doubles the violence—and is about the poorest excuse for intelligent action that thinking men ever have come up with. But understandably, the reason they always have come up with it, and continue to do so, is that they get into situations where they can't find anything else that gives a chance of working at all; there is nothing else *to* do. And it may very well be that, if one disregards the presence of a God of resurrection capability, the diagnosis is just exactly correct: man can get himself into situations where there *is* nothing else to do.

But because the suffering servant knows that there *is* a God in the picture, he *always* sees another alternative. The world's way of fighting violence with violence is, shall we say, *counterproductive*, so the servant's method will need to be a "reverse fighting." If he can manage to *absorb* the violence into himself rather than either responding with new violence of his own or hardening himself in a way that deflects the original violence back into the world, he has a means of damping the reaction and winding down the conflict. But of course, if what very likely *might* happen does happen and he gets more violence than he can endure, this ends his effectiveness as a fighter and isn't so good for his health, either. At that point, his method hardly can be said to have worked.

Here, then, is where God's resurrection is essential to the process. By "resurrection" we do not mean to identify anything too specific, and it may not be the most accurate term for what we have in mind. *God* is the one to say what form the "resurrection" will take, when and how it will happen. Recall that the biblical picture itself is flexible enough that it can accommodate Zion delivered at the very last moment, a return to Zion, a rebirth of Zion, a resurrection from death—they all have the same significance.

All that faith affirms is that, by resurrecting Jesus, God has shown us that he has the means for handling any situation. However, the believer does not try to tell God how and when he should use those means; his only responsibility, as servant, is to obey his orders and thus give God the opening he can use.

To use an analogy, the suffering servant is like an inflatable punch toy. He takes a terrific beating, and it isn't too difficult to knock him down. But he is so weighted at the bottom (with the mass of God's faithfulness) that he always bobs up again. Evil is stymied because it simply cannot get the usual chain reaction as much as started. It punches itself out against the defenselessness of the servant. In time, then, the situation arises which is described in Deutero's Suffering-Servant chapter: the kings finally come to the realization that they are not actually *punishing* the servant but that the suffering he bears is for *their* benefit. This leads to repentance and forgiveness. There is the difference, of course, that Servant Israel's suffering, rather than claiming any redemptive effect in and of itself, is a pointer and witness to the suffering of the one by whose scourging we truly *are* healed.

Sören Kierkegaard proposed an illustration that can carry our thought further. He spotted what we have called the "chain reaction effect" and likened it to a whirlpool or gyration. Each new action brings a reaction that has the effect of kicking the whirl into a faster and faster spin until it explodes into a shatter of atoms.

Kierkegaard observes that the usual way of trying to affect such a situation is to feed in a new power vector intended to bend the flow of force in the direction *we* think things ought to go. That is, we seek to manipulate the process toward what we envision as the desired outcome. However, he suggests, more often than not the insertion of *this* power factor merely arouses an escalated reaction from those who are trying to make things come out somewhere else, and the unintended effect is to give the spin another kick.

This would seem to describe the results of a number of the techniques that have been employed by anti-war groups. In some cases the intent seemed to be deliberately to accelerate the whirl under the theory that the shattering of the system is itself tantamount to peace—although this hardly is the biblical vision of peace coming as the fruit of love, reconciliation, and forgiveness. But more often the assumption surely is that peace can be created if only we bring into the situation some political pressures that will channel events in the direction we think right. And Kierkegaard would seem to be correct; very often these attempts to manipulate achieve nothing but to heighten the antagonisms and make the polarization more extreme.

No, Kierkegaard says, the only effective way to brake uncontrolled gyration is to introduce, not a new power vector, but *a fixed point.* A whirlpool quickly is dissipated when it hits a rock that refuses to whirl. The rock is not trying to use the whirlpool for its own ends, trying to make it come out a certain way, trying to beat it at its own game. No, the rock isn't trying to *do* anything except stand solidly in its God-given place. Nevertheless, by "reverse fighting" (i.e., by refusing to whirl rather than by fighting in the gyrational way that whirlpools do), the rock offers itself to be battered against, absorbing the spin energy into itself, and thus bringing the wild movement to a halt.

This would seem to be an apt analogy for the work of the suffering servant. He is not merely another politician, working for a somewhat different goal than the others, yet matching wits, schemes, and power against theirs. No, as a fixed point he is striving only to be unmovable in his obedience to the God whose servant he is. And this again is the point where a behind-the-scenes power on the order of a resurrection is essential to the picture. No person, on his own, is rock enough to keep from being whirled out of position by this world's suck and smash. His only hope of succeeding (indeed, his *guarantee* of succeeding) is that he is incorporate with the Rock of Ages—and that one just isn't about to be rolled aside by any big swish!

Now the objection most often raised against the suffering-servant idea is that it is spineless, weak, namby-pamby, and wishy-washy. It would ask us to become Caspar Milquetoasts.

Nonsense! The charge has no truth in it. Our model is Jesus of Nazareth—and if anyone thinks he can hang the Caspar Milquetoast label on *him* . . . well, he is welcome to try.

Perhaps the diametric difference is this: Milquetoast is the person who "won't stand up to anybody," who "lets people walk all over him," who "gets treated like a doormat." In the face of opposition he wilts; in fact, when he sees somebody coming at him, he is likely to lie down in readiness for being stepped on. And all of this, presumably, springs from a basic lack of self-respect or any sense of self-worth.

Quite the contrary, the suffering servant knows who he is and has complete respect for himself in regard to that identity—although not in any way that would signify vanity or pride over what he has made of himself. But he is aware that he has been called into the service of King Jesus, that he is known and supported by him, that he has been made a partner in the cause that is overcoming the world. Who has better grounds for self-respect than the servant?

And he is not anything like a doormat. It is true that neither the servant nor the doormat "fights back"—according to what the world means by fighting back. But the servant's assignment is precisely to *stand up* to the onslaught of evil rather than *lie down* before it. Indeed, the whole point of the "resurrection factor," upon which we have been insisting so strongly, is that the servant be able to hang in there, rather than getting rolled over or ridden out of the play. The servant's call to *absorb* punishment is not at all the same thing as *crumpling* under it.

In *The Day of His Coming*, a book about Jesus that gives strong support to much of what we have observed, Gerhard Gloege says that Jesus, in his career, combined two qualities which we tend to treat as contradictory. These are *resistance* and *submission*. Our rock-and-whirlpool analogy can help elucidate what Gloege has in mind. The rock *resists* the whirlpool in that it refuses to be washed aside. It *submits* to the whirlpool in that it makes no effort to act upon it, manipulate its flow, direct its course; the rock is content simply to be acted upon.

Just so, Jesus *resisted* in that he refused to let the world force him into its own mold; he took his position and would not be budged out of it. Yet, at the same time, he was entirely *submissive*. He made no effort to assert his power over others and did nothing to stop those who chose to punish him for not conforming. As far as protecting or defending himself, he was entirely submissive; as far as letting others dictate his position and stance, he was unmovable. And the implication is that his followers should be the same way.

We have called the servant's way "reverse *fighting*"—and we intend a certain literalness in the phrase. The Holy War rootage of the idea has not been renounced. To *stand* and take violence without either returning it in kind or collapsing before it—this is a very difficult stance to maintain and one that calls for strength of the highest order. It would seem to be the case that every quality of character traditionally glorified in the warrior also is required of the suffering servant—plus some qualities of patience, endurance, self-discipline, faith, hope, and love that are not necessarily part of the warrior picture. Once one has seen *the* Suffering Servant take his way to the cross, it becomes impossible to use the word "sissy" in this connection again.

There is one further consideration; we mentioned it earlier. Before, under, in, and through his suffering, the servant has been given the more "aggressive" duty of *serving* his fellowman. It is not his first call to be seeking out someone who will volunteer to beat on him; his suffering is not an end in itself. His first call is to be out serving the neighbor; but when that brings him into a situation of conflict, he is ready to meet it in his particular way.

In this regard it is accurate to say that the servant *chooses* his sufferings. Although his method is to *allow* the opponent to work his pleasure upon him, he retains a real degree of self-determination in that, under God's guidance, he decides through *which* suffering he can be of greatest service. It is not so much, then, that the violent ones *get* the servant under their power as that he deliberately *puts* himself there—and even then, not as an indication that they have defeated him, but that he is going to take their power from them . . . by absorbing it.

Thus, the New Testament word usually translated "servant"—but which more accurately ought to read "slave"—does not quite say all that needs to be said. A *slave* serves others because he *has* to; he has no other choice; the control of the situation lies entirely in the hands of the master. But, from Deutero on, this never has been the case of the Suffering Slave. Jesus assumed "the nature of a slave" (Philippians 2:7); he was among us "like a servant" (Luke 22:27); he performed slave labor for his disciples (the footwashing of John 13); but there is not the slightest suggestion that he was anything other than an entirely *free* man. He did not relinquish control into the hands of those whom he served or under whom he suffered. He *laid down* his life; it was not *taken from him* (John 10:17-18).

And so, too, every suffering servant enlisted by King Jesus is as free as the King himself, because the King guarantees that freedom. The suffering servant assumes the likeness of a slave and suffers as a slave because he *chooses* to, because this is the service he *wants* to perform for his King, his brethren, and the world.

7

The King Is in
His Accounting House

I know how hard pressed you are, and poor—and yet you are rich. . . . Do not be afraid of the suffering to come. . . . Only be faithful till death, and I will give you the crown of life. . . . He who is victorious cannot be harmed.
—King Jesus (Revelation 2:9-11)

Here we a ready for the wrap-up—and the Bible is kind enough to provide just what we need, namely, the book of Revelation.

We have no intention of doing anything like a thorough treatment of the book. (For that, I recommend my own full-length study, *The Most Revealing Book of the Bible.*) Here we merely will pick out a few major ideas and follow the one line of thought that serves our interest. In the process we will do some fancy sidestepping, selecting the verses we want and skipping over a multitude of others that cry out for explanation. However, we skip these, not because we are afraid of them, but because we don't want to get bogged down and distracted from our main goal. We will present our interpretation without even trying to *prove* that the book as a whole supports it.

What we will find in Revelation (you might guess) is the familiar Zion scheme. Yet that way of putting it is only half true.

The basic ideational pattern will be quite familiar; the terminology, point of view, and method of presentation will be new and different. What we have, then, is still another *variation* of the Zion tradition—or perhaps another *descendant* of the old Zion tradition—for we have indeed come a long way from where we started.

And yet we will discover that, in some ways, we have come full circle—thus making Revelation particularly appropriate as our wrap-up. For instance, we now will encounter a stronger and more militaristic Holy War imagery than we have seen since leaving Joshua, Deborah, and Gideon. Nevertheless, this is truly a *New Testament* book rather than a regression to Joshua-Judges. Revelation can remind us that our entire biblical journey indeed has been a unity.

However, the aspect in which the book is both most new and most appropriate as a wrap-up is its point of view. From the very beginning, of course, the Zion tradition has recounted an end-state oriented synopsis. That is, all of the prior steps of the sequence point toward and find their significance in the final outcome—which, in this instance, is the kingly rule of God with its accompaniment of justice and peace. This end-state, of course, is the be-all and end-all of the sequence as a whole.

The Old Testament prophecies, obviously, looked toward the end-state from a rather remote distance, standing some way in front of the near end of the chain of events and projecting the entire picture from there. The Gospels and epistles got much closer. They come from far down into the sequence itself and could proclaim the victory of Skull Hill as accomplished fact. Nevertheless, the end goal still had to be projected forward from that point. However, Revelation, in imagination (or in the Spirit), carries us into the end-state itself and lets us look backwards from *that* vantage. Thus the sequence as a whole is foreshortened so as to stand out with clarity and in its proper proportions—a most fitting wrap-up indeed.

We shall hop, skip, and jump our way through the book, putting our feet down on the spots that will support our weight and lead us to the goal on the other side.

> This is the revelation given by God to Jesus Christ. It was given to him so that he might show his servants what must shortly happen. He made it known by sending his angel to his servant John, who, in telling all that he saw, has *borne witness* to the word of God and to the *testimony* of Jesus Christ. . . . Grace be to you and peace, . . . from Jesus Christ, the *faithful witness*, the first-born from the dead and ruler of the kings of the earth.
>
> Revelation 1:1-2, 4-5; italics mine.

These opening verses are of great importance in that they—quite deliberately it would seem—introduce some of the basic concepts that underlie the book as a whole.

Notice, in the first place, that both the Christians to whom the book is addressed and the author himself are identified as *servants* (slaves) of Christ; and this usage is customary throughout. Primarily the phrase would suggest that a Christian is one who serves Christ. However, it also could signify one who, in the name of Christ, serves the needs of the world—which, certainly, is the way Christ instructs us to serve *him*. Undoubtedly both meanings are involved and should be preserved. In any case, at every point in the book and in its total impress, the Christian is represented as a servant—and, we shall discover, a servant who is destined to suffer. By looking only at one word, we have placed our thought squarely in the Zion tradition.

However, there is another word here that is even more significant. Each of the three italicized phrases in the text represents an appearance of the Greek root which has evolved into our English word "martyr." Its basic meaning is "witness" or "testimony"; and the way John uses the term makes it plain that he does not understand "witnessing to Jesus" to mean merely "talking about Jesus" but rather "living in such a way that one's whole demeanor reminds people of Jesus and points them toward him."

Yet we know that the English word "martyr" means "one
who is *killed* for the sake of his faith." How did this change of
meaning come about? The answer seems obvious. During the
period of early Christianity, the opposition of the world was such
that anyone who was a true and faithful *martyr* (witness) ran a
very high risk of being *martyred* (killed). The two situations
tended to coincide, and the meaning of the word sort of slid off
the one and onto the other. At the time of John's writing, the
word probably could point either way or both ways. And because
the fact of whether or not one actually *does* get killed is not the
crucial point—that event not lying within the control of the witness himself—perhaps the best way to define John's term is: "a
witness of such quality that the person gives his entire life to it and
is willing to accept death for it."

The last two occurrences of the term are of particular importance. The very last one, being significant as the first title the
book ascribes to Jesus, calls him "the faithful martyr-witness."
The term applies both ways. Of course, he did give his life for his
cause. But was he a *witness*? If so, to *what* did he witness? He witnessed to—his whole being was a witness to—the coming
kingdom of God, the new age, the new quality of life, the possibilities of universal peace, justice, and love that God intends for
and even now is offering to mankind. John's is not one of the
usual titles given to Jesus, but there is none more expressive of
what his life and ministry were all about.

The preceding occurrence of *martyr* is one that becomes a
specialized term for John, "*martyria Jesu.*" This can be translated
either as "the testimony (witness) *of* Jesus" or "the testimony (witness) *to* Jesus." When, as here, it is Jesus himself making the witness, the first meaning, of course, is intended—that is, it is Jesus'
own testimony to the coming kingdom of love and peace. But
when speaking of "Christ's servants," as John calls them, both
meanings of the phrase apply simultaneously. The Christians do
of course witness *to* Jesus, i.e., they live and act in such a way as to
direct attention to him. However, in so doing they also participate

in the witness *of* Jesus, standing for and directing attention to the reality to which he himself witnessed. "*Martyria Jesu*" can and should carry both meanings.

That Christians are, in the first place, "*servants* (slaves) of Christ" and, in the second place, *martyr witnesses* who witness both to Jesus and to the testimony of Jesus—these two designations catch up all that the rest of the Bible has developed regarding the suffering servant and add an important element which has not been made this clear previously. A martyr-servant is, obviously, a *suffering* servant. But now we see that the basic significance of his suffering is as a form of *witness*.

King Jesus recruits reverse fighters to follow him in defenseless suffering before the forces of violence and conflict. But it is not so much that *their* actions overcome the world as that they witness to King Jesus and, through him, to that to which he himself witnessed, namely, God's reconciling of all things unto himself. And truly, both Jesus' witness and mankind's witness thus have their part to play in God's making it happen.

The threefold title, which concludes the passage and which John undoubtedly chose with care as the means of introducing Jesus into his book, relates our line of thought to the Zion tradition as beautifully as anything could. Jesus is, first of all, "the faithful *martyr* (witness unto death)." This characterizes his role and ministry up to and including the cross. And although the matter is not made explicit at this point, the terminology opens the way for the witness of his martyr-servants in their turn.

Second, he is "the first-born from the dead." Precisely because of the faithfulness of his *martyr*dom, the victory over death is conferred upon him—in the resurrection, of course. And in this case, the wording, "*first*-born," makes it plain that the experience is not to stop with Jesus himself but is to extend to his martyr-servants in their turn.

Third, he is "ruler of the kings of the earth." Again, precisely because of his victory over death, he is exalted to a universal rule and lordship. And again, although it is not made explicit here,

later references will make it plain that his martyr-servants are to
share in that lordship. The reference to "the kings of the earth" is
particularly reminiscent of Deutero's Suffering-Servant passage,
for there, recall, it also was the kings of the earth who caused the
Servant to suffer and then beheld his exaltation over them.

It will become quite evident what special meaning these
kings of the earth have in John's mind (and likely had for Deutero
as well). They are commanders-in-chief of their respective armies,
the leaders and sponsors of military activity, and thus the very
symbols of the wars and fightings that constitute the prime
concern of our study. It will be most interesting and instructive to
follow through and discover what John does with these kings in
the course of his book—but it is significant that he introduces
them this early and in the way he does.

The author's introduction of himself forms an interesting
parallel (or complement) to his introduction of Jesus:

> I, John, your brother and joint-participant in the suffering and
> sovereignty and endurance of Jesus—I came to be on the island
> called Patmos because of the word of God and the *martyria Jesu*.
>
> Revelation 1:9 (my translation).

First, the fact that he is a brother and joint-participant along
with his fellow Christians indicates that what he says of himself is
by no means peculiar to his own experience but in the normal pattern for those who fight with King Jesus. Then that experience is
described not as something *independent* of Jesus' own history and
not even as a *recapitulation* of Jesus' history but actually as a *participation* in Jesus' history. That participation is treated under
three headings which are reminiscent of the three titles earlier as-
cribed to Jesus—although different enough to be interesting.

"The suffering" answers to Jesus' being "the faithful *martyr
witness.*" "The sovereignty" answers to Jesus' being "ruler of the
kings of the earth." John does not have a term answering to Jesus'
being "the first-born from the dead." However, it is difficult to

see how one could get from "the suffering" to "the sovereignty" without a resurrection of some sort; and elsewhere in the book he makes it clear that such is to be a part of the Christian's expectation.

Nevertheless, what John does use here as his third term constitutes a major contribution to his thought. The *patient endurance* of Jesus—his steadfastness and fortitude—is a quality his servants desperately need and one to which John gives frequent attention. It is an aspect of Jesus' history that is very relevant to the modern peace witness. Many contemporary peacemakers seem quite willing to go the way of the servant and accept suffering for their cause. But once they have tried this for awhile and there is no success, no coming of peace, they get frustrated and impatient. Then they either go AWOL or else try to hurry the process by introducing a little of strong-arm and manipulate-the-whirlpool tactics. They need what John sees as being a major element of the Christian experience, the *patient endurance* of Jesus.

Finally, John tells us that his own suffering, i.e., his being exiled to the Isle of Patmos, was occasioned by his preaching the word of God and his *martyria Jesu*. This last surely is meant both ways: as his witness *to* Jesus and his involvement in the witness *of* Jesus.

Following the introduction, John opens the body of the book with a vision of the heavenly Christ. One impressive feature of his description is that "out of his mouth came a sharp two-edged sword" (Revelation 1:16). This author is not afraid to identify Christ as a fighter—although he will introduce some other symbols that greatly qualify the nature of that fighting.

When the envisioned one speaks, his words are found to be of direct relevance to our study.

> Do not be afraid. I am the first and the last, and I am the living one; for I was dead and now I am alive for evermore, and I hold the keys of Death and [Hades].
>
> Revelation 1:17-18.

"Do not be afraid" is a line we met originally in the old Holy War tradition. That Jesus is "the first and the last" implies that he has control of the entire historical process. That he is "the living one" probably means to say more than that he simply is alive; he is himself the embodiment of *life*, the opponent and opposite of anything that tends toward dying and death. His status as "the living one," we are told, was accomplished through the crucifixion and resurrection, where he not merely faced and experienced death but, as it were, absorbed it into himself and came out victorious on the other side. As a consequence, he "holds the keys of Death and Hades," i.e., even though they have not been taken entirely off the scene as yet, he already possesses the wherewithal for putting these scoundrels behind bars once and for all. "Hades" is "the realm of death," or "whatever is of the order of death." Certainly, all that we have been designating as "wars and fightings" comes under this category. The passage deals directly with our topic.

What it comes to is that Jesus is *victor;* and "victory" is a major theme of the book of Revelation. Jesus regularly is presented as the victorious one—and his servants as those who in due course will become victorious with him. In this opening vision, the heavenly Christ dictates letters to each of the seven churches in John's locality there in Asia Minor. Each of the letters promises victory to those who remain loyal, but the last one, the one to Laodicea, says pointedly: "To him who is victorious I will grant a place on my throne, as I myself was victorious and sat down with my Father on his throne" (Revelation 3:21).

King Jesus *and* his followers both are to be victors, are to participate in the same victory; but there is an important difference. The follower's victory consistently is promised as a *future* reality, something yet to come. Jesus' is just as consistently described as an *accomplished* reality, something already done. Clearly, for the Revelator, the death-and-resurrection signifies *the* victory of Jesus. The consequences of that victory have not all worked themselves out yet; but there is absolutely no expectation of any further battle to be fought nor victory to be won by Jesus—nor would there be any place for such expectation. The already-accomplished victory is sufficient to turn the trick.

This interpretation undoubtedly runs contrary to what most people have assumed they know about Revelation, and we will need to test the thesis further as we proceed; but it has crucial implications regarding our particular interest. According to John, everything prerequisite to the disappearance of wars and fightings and the coming of the longed-for era of peace and justice already has taken place. Jesus' death and resurrection did it. In other words, the point at which we stand in the Zion cycle is not *before*, not even *on the verge of*, the decisive, delivering, liberating act of God. No, we stand *after* the victory itself but *before* the completion of its working out.

This means, for one thing, that King Jesus' followers, fighting in their reverse way, are fighting a war that is already won. This is not to say that their fighting lacks all significance; but it is to say that the issue is no way in doubt. "Yahweh *has given* the enemy into your hands!" And consider that, in a football game or any other sort of conflict, this is when the fighting really gets to be fun—after the game is won even if it isn't over. Far from becoming anxious and frustrated over the seeming intransigence of the industrial-military complex and the apparent impossibility of making any perceptible dent upon the world, the *Christian* peacemaker knows that the monster already has been decapitated by the sharp two-edged sword of Jesus.

"Swish" went Jesus with his good sword Death-and-Resurrection.

"Ha! You missed me," gloated the Dragon.

"Think so?" smiled Jesus. "Just wait until you try to turn your head."

And that's where we are. The servants of Jesus, in their martyr-witness, are merely keeping the pressure on a bit until the Dragon's head falls off. This does not mean that they won't have their share of suffering to absorb and a real need for the endurance of Jesus, but the war itself is as good as over in any case. This essentially is what the heavenly Christ says in his letter to the church at Smyrna:

> These are the words of the First and Last, who was dead and came to life again: I know how hard pressed you are, and poor—and yet you are rich.... Do not be afraid of the suffering to come. The Devil will throw some of you into prison, to put you to the test; and for ten days [i.e., a short period] you will suffer cruelly. Only be faithful till death, and I will give you the crown of life.
>
> Revelation 2:8-10.

By the way, these letters to the churches do themselves represent a very familiar phase of the traditional cycle. What we witness here is the Messiah *purging Zion:*

> But I have this against you: you have lost your early love. Think from what height you have fallen; repent, and do as you once did.... So repent! If you do not, I shall come soon and make war upon [you] with the sword that comes out of my mouth.... This will teach all the churches that I am the searcher of men's hearts and thoughts, and that I will reward each one of you according to his deeds.... I know all your ways; that though you have a name for being alive, you are dead. Wake up, and put some strength into what is left, which must otherwise die!... All whom I love I reprove and discipline. Be on your mettle therefore and repent.
>
> Revelation 2:4-5, 16, 23; 3:1-2, 19.

Following the heavenly Christ's dictation of the letters to the churches, the scene shifts to Mission Control Upstairs. John, the visitor, is in consternation because God holds a great scroll that is sealed with seven seals and yet no one can be found who is worthy to break the seals and look inside. Doubtless this scroll represents the unknown future of the world; and the problem is: Who or what can set history's course so as to decide the outcome of the human adventure? What will make the difference regarding the final result of the historical process, and who can say what that result will be?

One of John's guides tells him, "Do not weep; for the Lion from the tribe of Judah, the Scion of David, has won the right to open the scroll and break its seven seals" (Revelation 5:5). The language at this point follows an Isaiah model: it is militant ("the Lion"), royal, and messianic ("the Scion of David"); but it will change drastically in the very next verse. He *"has won* the right," that is, he did *something particular* to merit the prerogative, and that action is something already accomplished *in the past.*

The "Lion" then puts in his appearance; and lo and behold, he is "a Lamb with the marks of slaughter upon him" (Revelation 5:6). Here is the Revelator's most basic image of Christ. The model is from Deutero. "The Lamb" is probably deliberately reminiscent of Deutero's "he was led like a sheep to slaughter, like a ewe that is dumb before the shearers, without protection, without justice." It is a powerful symbol of self-giving defenselessness. That he bears the marks of slaughter indicates that he already has played through the role of innocent suffering to its bitter conclusion in martyrdom and death—and yet has gone *through* death, surmounted it, and become the Living One. And yet, the fact that, without contradiction, this Lamb *is* the Lion—surely this indicates that the Lamb's way of defenselessness is a true posture of *strength* and a means of *fighting and conquest.* John has made the Isaiah/Deutero combination, the Suffering-Servant Messiah, more graphic than has ever been done before.

Out of such passages as this, early Quaker thinkers developed a concept of "the Lamb's War." That particular phrase does not appear in Revelation (any more than "Holy War" appeared in Joshua-Judges); but the concept itself is true to a fundamental theme of the book: Christ's is a *reverse* way of fighting, which is yet the key to the conquest of all the world's evil.

As the Lamb takes the scroll and prepares to open it, he is greeted with a great hymn:

> *Thou art* worthy to take the scroll and to break its seals, for *thou wast* slain and by thy blood didst purchase for God men of every

tribe and language, people and nation: thou hast made of them a
royal house, to serve our God as priests; and *they shall* reign upon
earth.
Revelation 5:9-10; italics mine.

The sequence of verb tenses is important. Christ, right now, in
this very moment, *is* in control of the outcome of history because
of what he *did* at that time in the past; and as a consequence,
those who are his *shall* reign in the future. *His* past has established
the present power that guarantees *our* future.

The line about "men of every tribe and language, people
and nation" signifies that the Lamb's work is of a universal scope
which does not, *in principle*, exclude any person. The next line
makes it clear that the current duty of these people is "to serve our
God," presumably by fighting in the train of the Lamb and according to his methods.

The seven seals are then opened in turn, each one triggering
a particular vision. Two of these are significant for our purposes:

> When he broke the fifth seal, I saw underneath the altar the souls of
> those who had been slaughtered for God's word and for the
> testimony *[martyria (Jesu)]* they bore. They gave a great cry: "How
> long, sovereign Lord?" ... They were told to rest a little while
> longer, until the tally should be complete of all their brothers in
> Christ's service who were to be killed as they had been.
> Revelation 6:9-11.

"Underneath the altar" probably is intended to represent the
direct presence of God. But the essential point here is that the *one*
human activity which has significance regarding the ultimate victory over evil is, not the building of the great society, not the com-
bating of social evil, but the bearing of the suffering-servant
martyria Jesu, the making of the witness that goes defenselessly to
death. If this is what John means—and what else can he mean?—
he has made one of the most radical pronouncements in all scripture and one that calls into judgment by far the greater part of our
thought and action.

As the sixth seal is broken, the whole cosmos begins to dissolve into horror and trauma:

> Then *the kings of the earth,* magnates and marshals, the rich and the powerful, and all men, slave or free, hid themselves in caves and mountain crags; and they called out to the mountains and the crags, "Fall on us and hide us from the face of the One who sits on the throne and from the vengeance of the Lamb."
>
> Revelation 6:15-16; italics mine.

This vision, plainly, is presented as the antithesis of the one before, the souls of the martyrs played off against the kings of the earth. Obviously, John's list goes from the most awful bad to the not quite so bad; and the kings of the earth come in even a notch ahead of other military types. For John, war-making represents the most guilty guilt there is. And these characters know just what it is they have asked for and have got coming; they fully expect "the vengeance of the Lamb." Be that as it may, the fact that the avenger is *the Lamb* might suggest that his "vengeance"—like his "fighting"—could be of a rather strange sort (perhaps even a *reverse* vengeance of "Father, forgive them"?). We'll have to wait to find out; so continue to keep an eye peeled for "the kings of the earth."

At this point we skip to Revelation 11 to treat the passage of the book which may be most pertinent to our study. The vision takes place in Jerusalem, at the temple—which could signify a direct link to the Zion tradition:

> "I have two witnesses [martyrs], whom I will appoint to prophecy, dressed in sackcloth, all through these twelve hundred and sixty days." These are the two olive-trees and the two lamps that stand in the presence of the Lord of the earth. If anyone seeks to do them harm, fire pours from their mouths and consumes their enemies.
>
> Revelation 11:3-5.

Let us examine first the *character* of these two and then the

fact of their *twoness*. The details would point us toward identifying them as the church, the community of Christians. They are
"martyr witnesses"—the term John consistently has used in
reference to the church.

Their activity extends over the period of "twelve hundred
and sixty days"—to which John makes reference time and again.
Twelve hundred and sixty days (also appearing as forty-two
months and as three and a half years) is, most basically, three and
a half years. Throughout Revelation, "7" stands as God's number,
the "good" number. A "3½" is a *broken* "7" and thus consistently
the "bad" number, the number of Evil. The three and a half
years, then, regularly refers to that time during which Evil *seems*
to have taken control of the world, namely, the period running
from Evil's *apparent* victory in crucifying Jesus until Jesus' *true*
victory is made manifest by the removal of Evil. And this, of
course, is precisely the period throughout which the Christian
church is called to make its witness and suffer its martyrdom. (The
three and a half *days*, which we shall encounter in a bit, represent
the last, terrible intensification which will conclude the three and
a half *years*. It marks Evil's last-gasp struggle.)

The witnesses also are called olive-trees and lamps, that is,
they are to *bear fruit* and *give light*. How better could the task of a
servant-witness church be described?

John tells us that the witnesses are two; but he makes
absolutely no distinction between them, treating them in concert
throughout the story. This twoness may intend merely that discipleship is meant to be a *communal* activity—that Jesus knew it
proper to send out disciples two-by-two. However, what John
might well have seen as a basic twoness of the church would be
the distinction between congregations of Jewish background and
those of Gentile background. We tend not to be aware of how different these two must have appeared to observers on the scene.
Their distinctions likely were as numerous and striking as those,
say, between a black Baptist congregation and a white Roman
Catholic congregation today. But if this explanation is correct,

then John pictures *two* witnesses as a way of stressing that the *entire* church shares the calling of servant, martyr-witness discipleship.

That the witnesses spit out fire to consume their enemies likely should not be understood to contradict the basic theme which the Revelator has been developing. After all, as the story continues, these witnesses do become true martyrs in the likeness of Jesus himself. More probably, John means to portray them as rocks in a whirlpool. They will not let themselves simply be rolled aside; they do resist being ridden out of the play; and God does preserve them until they have had opportunity to make their testimony and until the time is right for them to go on in submission to death.

> But when they have completed their testimony [*martyria*], the beast that comes up from the abyss will wage war upon them and will defeat and kill them. Their corpses will lie in the street of the great city, whose name in allegory is Sodom, or Egypt, where also their Lord was crucified. For three days and a half men from every people and tribe, of every language and nation, gaze upon their corpses and refuse them burial. All men on earth gloat over them, make merry, and exchange presents; for these two prophets were a torment to the whole earth. But at the end of the three days and a half the breath of life from God came into them; and they stood up on their feet to the terror of all who saw it. Then a loud voice was heard speaking to them from heaven, which said, "Come up here!"
>
> Revelation 11:7-12.

This scene is as explicit a rendition of Zion devastated but then miraculously preserved or restored as any in the Old Testament prophets. Quite plainly, we are told that, as history comes to its climax, the witnessing community will, in its own experience, reiterate the death and resurrection of its Lord. The specific little reminder that the scene takes place in the same city "where also their Lord was crucified" makes the interpretation as much as certain.

From earlier books of the New Testament we learned that

individual servants of Christ, in their own respective times, are to
fight in King Jesus' way, expect suffering, accept death, and
depend upon a resurrection. Here the pattern is applied on a
broader scale. In the Lamb's War, the disciple community as a
whole is to follow in his train; and it is through the resurrection *of
the Zion community* that the Lamb's Skull-Hill victory is completed as victory for the world.

There is real food for thought here. Goodness knows, few
enough individual Christians have borne their suffering-servant
witness to the testimony of Jesus. But historically, it may be that
the institutional church has an even poorer record. For the most
part, the church simply has not been a defenseless, self-expending
servant of mankind—and has pursued even her *peacemaking*
ministry as a rather strident, demanding, lecturing moral-instruc-
tor to the world. Of course, the church *can't* be what she ought to
be except as individual Christians make up their minds to be suffering servants, too. But we need to be working the Lamb's War
on both fronts: in our own lives and in the life of the olive-tree/
lamp community.

In Revelation, the author's line of approach is a circling one
that time and again comes back to describe the same events and
periods using different symbols and imagery. In Chapter 12,
again, appears an impressive hymn celebrating the Lamb's victory both in its initial accomplishment and its final completion:

> This is the hour of victory for our God, the hour of his sovereignty
> and power, when his Christ comes to his rightful rule! For the ac-
> cuser of our brothers is overthrown, who day and night accused
> them before our God. By the sacrifice of the Lamb they have con-
> quered him, and by the testimony [*martyria*] they uttered; for they
> did not hold their lives too dear to lay them down.
>
> Revelation 12:10-11.

The hour of sovereignty and power in which the victory of
Christ comes into its rightful recognition happens through his
followers. "The accuser of our brothers" is the great dragon,

Satan, the symbol of all that threatens mankind. The Christians conquer him, we are told, by the Lamb's self-sacrifice which already has been made, by their testimony to it, and by their putting their lives where he put his. This is the way in which John sees all evil—including, surely, wars and fightings—being overcome.

Another vision, this one in Chapter 14, makes a similar point but also ties into the Zion tradition and adds an important new insight at the same time:

> Then I looked, and on Mount Zion stood the Lamb, and with him were a hundred and forty-four thousand who had his name and the name of his Father written on their foreheads. . . . These are the men who did not defile themselves with women, for they kept themselves chaste, and they follow the Lamb wherever he goes. They have been ransomed as the firstfruits of humanity for God and the Lamb.
>
> Revelation 14:1, 4.

The mention of the Lamb on Zion certainly must be understood as an echo of the long-standing Zion tradition, with the Messiah as the city's king. In John's eyes, a hundred and forty-four thousand probably would have appeared as a very large number rather than the comparatively small one that it appears to us. More than that, it is a great big number, impressive in its wholeness and symmetry; it consists of twelve twelves (twelve squared) and that multiplied *a thousand times*. Still more, "12" is itself the particular number of Zion. In Chapter 21, where the Revelator describes in detail the appearance and *measurements* of the New Jerusalem (Zion) which is the church, the bride of the Lamb, every figure he gives is either a twelve or a twelve-based number (the "12" of the twelve tribes of the old Israel and the twelve apostles of the new). The hundred and forty-four thousand met here is the fitting complement to the glory of the victorious Lamb himself.

The description that follows probably has nothing whatever

to do either with their sex or the character of their sexual relationships. Throughout the Old Testament the custom is to
describe idolatry and unfaithfulness to God as if it were a case of
sexual infidelity. Likely John means to say nothing more than that
these are people who have been completely loyal to Christ and
have not gone chasing after other gods and god-substitutes.

The crucial phrase (which substantiates the above interpretation) is that "they follow the Lamb wherever he goes." Where the
Lamb goes, of course, is on the way of defenseless suffering,
death, and resurrection. Their way must be the same.

The concluding line introduces a new and striking thought.
The death-and-resurrection of the Lamb's followers does not have
significance only for them, as though the rest of mankind simply
were left high and dry (or perhaps deep and hot). Not at all; these
loyal followers are the *firstfruits* of humanity. And "firstfruits" (a
long established biblical concept) refers to the very first fruit to
appear in an orchard or the first part of any crop. This produce
was valued as itself being an announcement and guarantee of the
great harvest coming in its train. The Lamb's cohorts are fighting
not simply—or even primarily—for their own deliverance; theirs
is a war to liberate humanity.

In Chapter 16, John uses a series of seven "bowl visions" to
recount the final victory and the events leading up to it. At Bowl
Six, four spirits are dispatched from the Unholy Trinity of the
dragon, the beast, and the false prophet:

> They were sent out to muster all the kings of the world for the great
> day of battle of God the sovereign Lord.... So they assembled the
> kings at the place called in Hebrew Armageddon.
>   Revelation 16:14, 16.

Be alert; here are those kings of the earth again; and
wouldn't you guess on which side they are ready to fight! They
are the first line of volunteers in the Devil's army. "Armageddon"
may mean "the mount of assembly" and be a reference to a

passage in Isaiah 14 (see page 76 above) which presents a Nimrodian, Babel-like picture of Evil gathering its forces on a mountain to challenge the God of heaven. In any case, there would seem to be only one thing that could follow these verses, namely, the description of a great and decisive battle between the mustered forces of Evil and the defending forces of Good. The setup hardly could allow anything else.

And yet the lines immediately following those quoted are these: "Then the seventh angel poured his bowl on the air; and out of the sanctuary came a loud voice from the throne, which said, "It is over!" (Revelation 16:17).

What do you mean "It is *over!*"? It was only just ready to begin! What if somebody tried to have a war and the other side declared it won without even coming? There is no suggestion that an army of God even takes the field. Here, "Yahweh *has given* the enemy into your hands" has been taken to the furthest extreme. This, indeed, is a mystery. John is going to go through it again in another place and give us a few more clues.

Chapter 19 is the place:

> Then I saw heaven wide open, and there before me was a white horse; and its rider's name was Faithful and True, for he is just in judgment and just in war. His eyes flamed like fire, and on his head were many diadems. Written upon him was a name known to none but himself, and he was robed in a garment drenched in blood. He was called the Word of God, and the armies of heaven followed him on white horses, clothed in fine linen, clean and shining. From his mouth there went a sharp sword . . . . Then I saw the beast and the kings of the earth and their armies mustered to do battle with the Rider and his army. The beast was taken prisoner, and so was the false prophet.
>
> Revelation 19:11-15, 19-20.

It goes without saying that we have moved back into Holy War language and that full strength. However, bear in mind that elsewhere in the New Testament we have encountered Holy War talk yet discovered that the author was not deserting the suffering-servant pattern but merely affirming that suffering-servanthood truly can be a means of "fighting" (*reverse* fighting). The picture here is the most paradoxical of them all; but, we will maintain, it is of a kind with the others. In short, although the Rider, King Jesus, is pictured as a man of war, he is still the Lamb; John does *not* jump the track and introduce a strange, new Christ for one moment in the middle of his nineteenth chapter.

In the first place, this is another case of the battle that doesn't come off. We get even closer to it this time, in that the forces of Good as well as the forces of Evil are in place for a confrontation. Our quotation does skip several verses at the ellipsis; but these do not describe a military encounter—and obviously could not, because even the *presence* of an enemy force (including, take note, "the kings of the earth") is not recognized until the verse following. Some of the omitted verses (both from the middle of our quotation and after it) are quite bloody and warlike. However, they describe not a battle being fought to decide the issue but the mopping-up operations that follow a battle already won. Some of the phraseology is taken from the Old Testament; none of it *has* to be understood literally as physical violence against human beings. In this regard, continue to keep close tabs on "the kings of the earth." Although it would seem that they are killed and eaten by vultures at this point, we haven't heard the last of them yet.

However, if John intended to recount a decisive battle, it would about have to come between the last two sentences of our text. Yet it isn't there, and there is no space for it; the only thing appearing between those two sentences is a verse number.

So, if we don't have a battle, what under the sun do we have? We have a picture of a sudden, totally unexpected, inexplicable *capitulation* of the enemy. But why? What could cause it? Rather plainly, it is the very appearance of the Rider in his blood-drenched garment that causes it. There is no sense in fighting once you see that you are up against the fellow who already has whipped you hands down, once for all. If *he* is back, then there just isn't anything to be done!

The garment drenched in blood is the key. It customarily has been taken as just one gory detail out of the whole gory battle scene. However, if that is the case, then John has slipped and slipped badly. It is as plain as day; we are told about the bloody garment *before* there is any possibility of engagement with the enemy (the engagement that didn't quite come off anyhow). The Rider comes *to* the battlefield—more precisely, to the field which seemed ready to become a battlefield—with the blood *already upon* his garment. And Revelation has not recounted any previous engagement of which this blood could have been the consequence.

Nevertheless, we contend that this is indeed the blood of victory, the blood of a hard-fought, hard-won victory that was decisive for the outcome of the world. How so?

Although the imagery might be misleading, it is the conclusion of the *Lamb's* War that John is recounting. King Jesus, the Rider, is the Lamb; and the Lamb, recall, is one "with the marks of slaughter upon him." Inevitably, a slaughtered Lamb is going to get blood on his clothing. The blood that has drenched the garment of the Rider-Lamb is the blood of Skull Hill. And the victory of Skull Hill, which the Lamb won by giving his own life rather than by taking the lives of his enemies, is *the* victory that overcomes the world and eventuates now in the final capitulation of Evil. Once the enemy forces realize *who* the Rider is and are reminded by his blood-drenched garment of what he did to them at Skull Hill, the war is over.

There is but *one* war, the Lamb's War. There is but *one* King Jesus, the Rider who is, always has been, and always will be the Lamb. There is but *one* victory, that of Skull Hill. There is but *one* way of fighting, that of giving one's blood for shedding rather than shedding the blood of one's enemies.

If this interpretation be true—and certainly it fits much better with the rest of John's picture than customary interpretations of this passage do—then the tragedy of Christendom is revealed for what it is. How tragic that Christians, who have been enlisted into the war which is directed toward the ultimate capitulation of all evil and which war is, in fact, already won—how tragic that they should lose faith in the Lamb's way and resort to means of fighting that actually give aid and comfort to the enemy!

As the conclusion of his book, John draws for us a picture of the world that shall be after the Lamb's work is complete. It is the counterpart of the great era of peace and justice that the Old Testament prophets had drawn earlier, although John's picture is done on a grander scale, is more wonderful, and shows deeper insight:

> Then I saw a new heaven and a new earth, for the first heaven and the first earth had vanished, and there was no longer any sea. I saw the holy city, new Jerusalem, coming down out of heaven from God, made ready like a bride adorned for her husband. I heard a loud voice proclaiming from the throne: "Now at last God has his dwelling among men! He will dwell among them and they shall be his people, and God himself will be with them. He will wipe every tear from their eyes; there shall be an end to death, and to mourning and crying and pain; for the old order has passed away!" Then he who sat on the throne said, "Behold! I am making all things new!"
>
>   Revelation 21:1-5.

That the new earth centers in a new *Jerusalem* would indicate that we are winding up with what we first encountered early on, namely, a version of the Zion tradition. Notice that, although the city is heavenly in origin, its location is *on earth;* neither John nor the Bible as a whole is inclined to scratch off earth as a lost cause and go for a salvation which simply yanks privileged individuals out of the burning and up to some earth-free realm. No, the Bible *values* God's creation; and the gospel is pointed toward "the making of all things new," the recycling of creation and the salvaging of humanity—not the discarding of the world and the breaking up of mankind.

This consideration is of utmost importance, because it means

that our life upon earth, our service, our witness, our participation
in the Lamb's War, all have significance regarding the outcome of
history and the destiny of the race; they are not things that will
just be overruled and canceled out in a junk-piled creation.

John also beats the earlier dreamers all hollow when he
makes it plain that the heart of the new existence lies not so much
in magic new furniture and appliances as in a new quality of personal relationship, namely, man's reconciliation with God. "Now
at last God has his dwelling among men! He will dwell among
them and they shall be his people." To put the same thing a bit
differently: "The eastward jag of Adam, Cain, Nimrod, Babel,
and all, finally has been corrected and the race brought back to
center. Men no longer are trying either to hide from God or to
take his place. He is *with* them, and they are *his* people—sweet-
stepping, high-kicking ballerinas one and all."

Of course, it follows that there no longer is a "wherefrom"
from where wars and fightings *could* come. And the noted fact
that every tear is wiped and that death, mourning, crying, and
pain are no more—this cannot mean anything but that every sort
of war and fighting has disappeared as well. John portrays
everything we have been looking for.

Several verses later, he describes some interesting details
concerning the new Jerusalem:

> I saw no temple in the city; for its temple was the sovereign Lord
> God and the Lamb. And the city had no need of sun or moon to
> shine upon it; for the glory of God gave it light, and its lamp was the
> Lamb. By its light shall the nations walk, and the kings of the earth
> ["WHO?"] shall bring into it all their splendor. The gates of the city
> shall never be shut by day—and there will be no night.
> Revelation 21:22-25.

"There's got to be some mistake! The kings of the earth . . .
HERE? I don't believe it. Man alive; if that gang can make it,
then anybody can! How can this be?"

Frankly, we don't know *how* this can be—except to say that

with our Lamb nothing is impossible and that his victory is of a
magnitude that we who know only *military* victories can't even
begin to imagine. With us, the victory of the good guys always
means the defeat and destruction of the bad guys. But when the
winner is King Jesus, he brings the losers—even those God-
damned (so we had assumed) kings of the earth, and them in all
their splendor—right into the victory circle with him. "And if that
gang can make it, then anybody can." That's right—just exactly
right! The presence of those kings in the new Jerusalem means
that, in principle, we cannot deny the possibility of *any* person
turning up there.

Now there are some characters who John does not put into
the new Jerusalem and who, in principle, cannot appear there.
These are the dragon, the beast, the false prophet, death and
Hades, the principalities, the powers, and whatever. These are
embodiments of evil itself; and they must be overcome and
destroyed; there is nothing redeemable in them. But they are not
men. Men are *not* the enemy—even those men who, like the
kings of the earth, most closely have allied themselves with and
fought in the train of the enemy. The Lamb's War is fought *for*
man and against anything that is the enemy of man—including
the enemy within himself and the one to which he mistakenly has
given his allegiance. But man himself is not the enemy; and
therefore the gates of the city always are open *to man*.

"The gates of the city shall never be shut by day—and there
will be no night." We have come full circle, for here is something
the exact opposite of the city that Cain built in his effort to create
security for himself. His city—and, in principle, all the cities of
man—was built with *walls* and with gates that could be *shut* as a
means of keeping out the enemy (those bad people who are bent
on getting me). But because, through the Lamb's War, the true
enemy has been eliminated and the means provided for bad
people to become good, there is perfect security. Here indeed is
the only true security, namely, that which God *gives* rather than
what man cobbles together for himself. And its symbol is not the

city shut up tight to keep other men out, but the city whose gates are never closed, an invitation for men to *enter*.

Because we have been so emphatic about what John *does* say, perhaps it would be helpful to point out what he expressly does *not* say. (a) He does not say that there are no truly evil people, that everyone—by nature—is good enough to qualify for the new Jerusalem. Not at all; in fact, he deliberately protects himself against such a reading. Following our previous quotation about the open gates of the city, he immediately specifies: "But nothing unclean shall enter, nor anyone whose ways are false or foul, but only those who are inscribed in the Lamb's roll of the living" (Revelation 21:27). That seems clear enough.

(b) John does not say that there is no place for *punishment* in God's plan, that justice can be effected without the use of punishment. Not for a minute. Even though we now see these "kings of the earth" entering the city, John earlier had shown them being killed by the sword, being eaten by vultures, and then going into the lake of fire which is the second death. There is no question of the kings getting off easier than anyone else; and John cannot be accused of overlooking the necessity and rightness of punishment. If the kings are in the city, it is not because they have "gotten away with something." They will have come there the same way any of the rest of us sinners will—indeed, the same way the kings of Deutero-Isaiah *did*, by confessing that "he was pierced for our transgressions . . . and by his scourging we are healed."

(c) John does not say that we know for a fact that all men eventually will be saved. That would be claiming more knowledge of God's secret wisdom than he has offered to reveal. But neither does John say (nor, I believe, *would* he say) that we know for a fact that some people will *never* be saved and that we can have an idea as to who those people are. Jesus' Skull-Hill victory and the power of his resurrection are such that it hardly is for us to name limits beyond which they cannot reach or a time when their effect must cease. In short, if God's city is open-gated (as John tells us it is), we had best keep it that way—leaving it entirely to

God's decision as to who all will or will not eventually wash their robes and find admittance. John's final beatitude is "Happy are those who wash their robes clean! They will have the right to the tree of life and [may be entering] by the gates of the city" (Revelation 22:14, literal emendation). I do not find there any limit either stated or implied.

No, the city of peace and security where God himself dwells with his people—the open city that invites the entrance of man, even the kings of the earth, anyone who chooses to have his name inscribed in the Lamb's roll of the living—this is the spoil for which we fight!

8

Noticing the Absence
of What Wasn't There

*The madness, the frenzy, the boiling blood and the smoking brow, with
which, for a thousand lowerings old Ahab has furiously, foamingly chased
his prey—more a demon than a man!—aye, aye! what a forty year's fool—
fool—old fool, has old Ahab been!*
—Captain Ahab contemplating his obsessive passion for killing the
White Whale (in Herman Melville's *Moby Dick*)

When reading a book, any book, including the Bible (and
perhaps *particularly* the Bible) it is very important to take note not
only of what *is* said but also of what *is not* said. As readers, we
tend to come to a book with some preconceived ideas about the
subject at hand. Assuming that the author will be intelligent
enough to agree with us, we take for granted that the book will
say the things we are ready to hear. Sometimes we are so sure of
this that we finish the book supposing that it *did* say—or at least
meant to say—that which it deliberately did *not* say. Particularly
regarding the Bible do we often assume that we already know
what it should say, what it wants to say, and what, presumably, it
has said. In such case, then, it is a matter of great importance for
us to take careful note of the absence of what wasn't actually
there. So this chapter is legitimate Bible study—the study of what
the Bible doesn't say.

Of course, we do have in mind *a particular thing* that the Bible doesn't say. If the Bible *did* say it, the logical place for it to have done so would be in the book of Revelation; so let us examine its absence there. However, this absence also is to be found at all other places as well; the total silence should be understood as massive support for our interpretation.

Revelation, of course, speaks much about the dragon, the beast, and the false prophet—and about all the nasty, no-good "powers" employed by them. A good many of these "powers" are related to what currently is referred to as "our oppressive, sexist, racist, militaristic, dehumanizing society."

(However, it also should be noted that there are many of these "powers" that operate *within* persons, on an individual basis, rather than showing themselves primarily as "social problems." And for some strange reason—perhaps the activity of the "powers" themselves—Christians tend to divide up into two camps: one very aware and concerned about the "powers" of one manifestation and apparently oblivious to the others; the other group vice versa.)

Nevertheless, regarding the "societal powers"—of which, certainly, the wars and fightings of our present concern are dominant—the assumption seems to be that the Christian is called to track these monsters down to their lairs within our social system and there lay siege to them, cutting off their supplies, burning them out, slitting their throats, and generally doing them in. In short, it is assumed that King Jesus' first order of command is that his followers be engaged in effecting *social change.* "Political action" would seem to be the proper term—using this in the broad sense to include any and all activity directed at modifying the structures and policies of "the world," that is, of society at large.

However, even though the central theme of Revelation is the winning of the world, the conquest and elimination of the monsters, nowhere—nowhere at all—is there a statement, hint, implication, or insinuation that Jesus' followers are called to initiate action against these "powers." Such a call and such action would seem to be so completely natural and right, so "expected" in John's overall picture, that the absence must be an item for deep questioning and consideration. Time and again John *does* warn Christians to *resist* the powers, to avoid being captured or taken by them; but this is something quite different from a call to *pursue* them.

Likewise, if we recollect, we must realize that neither the suffering-servant pattern, the rock-in-the-whirlpool analogy, nor the martyr-witness concept gives any place for political initiative. What we would be inclined to think is basic and central is, in fact, totally lacking—and this must give us pause.

Well, then, why don't we find the call to political initiative? Why should Scripture be leery about inviting us to combat the powers, to go on a dragon hunt? Perhaps it is the case that a grave danger is involved—and not a danger to our *lives* obviously (our study has revealed anything but fear in that regard) but a danger to our *faith*. Perhaps it is the danger so graphically portrayed in Herman Melville's novel, *Moby Dick*.

Recall the story. Captain Ahab, a skilled and veteran seaman, commands the whaler *Pequod* out of nineteenth-century Nantucket. On a voyage previous to the opening of the story he had had a run-in with a great white whale and gotten his leg "devoured, chewed up, crunched by the monstrousest parmacetty that ever chipped a boat." The whale was given the name Moby Dick. On the present voyage, then, Ahab is out to accomplish but one thing, the destruction of the white whale.

As the story transpires, it becomes plain that Melville means for Moby Dick to represent more than just an extraordinarily large and vicious whale. He comes to be seen as an epitome of Evil—almost the equivalent of the Revelator's dragon or antichrist—and Ahab's is the obsession to rid the world of this malignity.

Ahab uses the *Pequod* to chase the white whale from ocean to ocean. He passes up many other whales he could have taken. He drives his ship and men through all sorts of trials and dangers.

His officers try to remind him that he has deserted the charge for which the shipowners employed him, namely, the acquiring of oil and whalebone. But Ahab will not listen; he *has* to get Moby Dick.

Toward the end—in the speech quoted as the headnote of this chapter—Ahab admits that, although his goal, the destroying of evil, seemed to be good, his effort was in actuality a demonic passion. But still he cannot stop. Finally, in a climactic and horrible encounter with the whale, Ahab lets himself, his crew, the ship—everything—be lost.

His last words are:

> Towards thee I roll, thou all-destroying but unconquering whale; to the last I grapple with thee; from hell's heart I stab at thee; for hate's sake I spit my last breath at thee.

And Melville, with great insight, leaves it inconclusive as to whether Moby Dick survives or not. That ultimately is not important. The point is that men can be captured and ruined by Evil as much by hating it and hunting it down as by loving it and hunting it out. Indeed, it may have been some such thought that led the prophet Isaiah to suggest that human beings simply are not good enough, wise enough, or strong enough to fight a Holy War. Certainly Ahab's action does betray a strong Nimrodian inclination toward trying to be *like God*.

And there would seem to be evidence in our day that some Christians have become so wholly motivated by a hatred of war, injustice, and establishment wickedness that they have slipped from the love and patience of the Suffering Servant into something more reminiscent of a Captain Ahab. But those who take it upon themselves to grapple with the U.S. government, for example, run the danger of taking on the likeness of the very thing they thought to oppose.

With Captain Ahab's *crusade* to eliminate Moby Dick—so different from Jesus' way against Evil—we are perhaps bringing into focus something that has been implied virtually throughout our study, namely, that all peace efforts divide naturally into two categories. And that little word "crusade" can help us get a hold on the idea we want. Implying, as it does, the zeal of an all-out organizational effort, being willing to use whatever means necessary to get the job done, it constitutes an accurate description of Ahab's activity. Yet what we do not often consider (and what most people don't even know) is that, etymologically, the word "crusade" actually means "cross-bearing." The word developed as a reference to the Crusaders who, between the 11th and 14th centuries, under the sign of the cross, fought "holy wars" against Islam.

Yet it must be obvious to everybody that the biblical concept of "cross-bearing" (applying that not alone to Jesus' crucifixion but to everything from Deutero's Suffering Servant through the command for us to take up our cross daily) is as different from a "crusade" as is day from night. Nevertheless, it is not difficult to spot the rationale that moves us from "cross-bearing" to "crusading."

Cross-bearing proceeds from the assumption that God is present as both sponsor and worker of the project in progress. God does call *us* to participate by taking up our crosses; but this is for our sakes, because he wants us to have the blessing of being involved, not because, for his own sake, God *must* have our help or else see his project come to naught. Clearly, this does not mean that it makes no difference whether the cross-bearer responds or not; it is not for a "draftee" to dictate the conditions of his service.

However, because the cross-bearer knows that the success of the effort lies with God rather than with himself ("Yahweh has given the enemy into your hands"), he can afford to remain calm and patient no matter how things seem to be going. Even when the situation gets desperate, he is not tempted to resort to tactics more promising than the defenseless suffering which God assigned him. His concern is totally with *fidelity* to his call. The *success* of his efforts can be left entirely to God, because he knows

that, even in case of total wipe-out, God still possesses the capability of resurrection victory.

Quite the contrary, a crusade shows the character it does
precisely because—no matter what lip service may go on—God is
not really trusted as being in charge. The assumption is that, if
things are to happen as they should, it will *have* to be the crusaders
themselves who make it so; it is their efforts that will determine
the outcome. And thus it turns out that, in face of threat,
"patience" simply will not serve and the mentality *must* be "let's
go all out, with whatever has to be done." And under this
premise, even *peace* crusades inevitably drift toward violence of
one variety or another.

With this distinction between Jesus' "cross-bearing" and
Captain Ahab's "crusading," we have come, then, to our two
basic categories of peacemaking. We shall call them the ESCHA-
TOLOGICAL and the SECULAR—but please do not draw any
conclusions from the words themselves until we have had opportunity to define them. It is most important that we protect the
terminology from misunderstanding. In particular, ours is not a
distinction simply between church-related activity and that not so
related; much, even, of what goes on inside churches will finally
have to be qualified as "secular." Neither is ours a distinction
between Christians and non-Christians; people who call themselves "Christians" are to be found in both groups, and the name
of Jesus very well may be invoked in both. Likewise, there are
concepts of "God" that will accord very nicely with what we are
calling "the secular," so the distinction cannot be simply that
between believers and atheists. Our categories are more subtle
and less obvious than any of these; so we will need to be careful in
understanding them.

The English word "secular" is derived from the Latin word
for "century" or "age," thus denoting "that which is of this age."
In particular, we shall use "secular" as referring to "what can be
accomplished *through human resources* within the limits of history *as we know it.*" The assumption is that historical possibility

includes nothing more than what human wisdom and technique can make of it.

The word "eschatological," on the other hand, comes from the Greek word for "end" or "goal" and denotes "thought and activity that is *end-state oriented*, directed toward a goal that lies beyond the potential simply of this age."

"Cross-bearing"—both because it is done entirely at the behest and under the aegis of the God who is *lord of history* and because it looks toward a resurrection lying beyond *historical possibility*—clearly is *eschatological*. And just as clearly, "crusading"—because, essentially, it represents this-worldly, apple-knowledge technique seeking this-worldly accomplishment—is *secular*. The secularist, of course, *believes* he is operating out of a total view of reality. Yet, in the eyes of an eschatologist, the secular perspective inevitably is seen as partial and constricted.

This observation enables us to exemplify the secular/eschatological relationship with a diagram—one that you better can draw in your mind's eye than I can on paper. Begin by making an X to mark the spot on which stands "the secularist." Around him draw a circle (as large or small as seems right) circumscribing "the present age," "this world," "history as we know it." And recall that, within this circle, along with the secularist, are to be found the institutional church, an understanding of Jesus, that which can be called "God," and a particular concept of Christianity—all of which a true eschatologist would deem "partial" yet have to recognize as "actual" for all that.

The trick of this diagram, then, lies in *not* making a new X upon which to place "the eschatologist." Most of all, that eschatologist is *not* to be put outside the secular circle. All tendencies to make the diagram represent two distinct and separate spheres are to be firmly resisted. It is not to be suggested, for instance, that the secularist is one who centers his existence upon *earth* while the eschatologist centers his upon *heaven*, the secularist upon *the physical* and the eschatologist upon *the spiritual*, the secularist upon *the present* and the eschatologist upon *the future*, or anything of the sort. Our distinction does not lie in any kind of "dualism."

No, the eschatologist is to be placed on the very same X with the secularist; there is no distinction as to *location* at all. The difference is that the secularist's horizon simply does not exist for the eschatologist. He sees right over it, past it, through it—state it as you will; represent it graphically if you can. And it is not that the eschatologist pierces that horizon at just one point or only in one direction; no, the horizon simply disappears. Thus, the eschatologist can see *back* to what were *God's purposes* in creating the world in the first place (as a stage for dancing with his ballerina) while the secularist cannot even see that there was a God there who had purposes. The eschatologist can look *around* to see a non-horizoned God who has acted within history and who presently is acting so, while the secularist, at best, can call "God" only something from within the horizon, something much too small and too weak for a real God. And the eschatologist can see *ahead* to God's promises and commitments regarding where history is to *come out*, while the secularist cannot see that history even has "a coming out." The eschatologist can see all that the secularist sees *and more;* but because he does see *more*, he also will *understand* quite differently the secular reality that the two of them see together. A chapter read as part of a longer novel will render a much different sense than if it be read as though it were meant for a short story, complete in itself.

Deutero-Isaiah, indeed, pegs the truth of Yahweh's being God precisely upon this understanding of eschatology:

> Let them come forward, these idols,
> Let them foretell the future.
> Let them declare the meaning of past events
>   that we may give our minds to it;
> let them predict things that are to be
>   that we may know their outcome.
> Declare what will happen hereafter;
> then we shall know you are gods.

> See how the first prophecies have come to pass,
>   and now I declare new things;
> before they break from the bud I announce them to you.
>
> Here and now I will do a new thing;
>   this moment it will break from the bud.
>   Can you not perceive it?
>
> > Isaiah 41:22-23a; 42:9; 43:19a.

Above, our use of the term "horizon" was intended to point us to an analogy that will further our thought. The secularist, now, is to be identified as "a flatlander," i.e., a person who believes that the earth is flat. The eschatologist, conversely, is "a round-earther" who knows that it is a sphere.

The secular assumption regarding the limits of life and history is in its own way as obvious and natural as was the original assumption that the earth is flat: within the everyday horizon of our human finitude, that is precisely how things "look." Nevertheless, the discovery that the world actually is round did not have to await the eschatologist's being lifted up and off his "X" to where he could see the curvature of the earth beyond the horizon. No, the discovery was made from the very same spot, seeing the very same things that secular flatlanders could see and always had seen. What the eschatological round-earther had learned was to interpret correctly the evidence of astronomical movements or of ships "sinking" out of sight below the horizon. All he had to do was "see" what everyone had been "looking at"; the whole time, the world itself had included signals trying to tell him that its "horizon" was an illusion.

Just so, becoming a Christian eschatologist does not involve being lifted out of this world into some transcendent realm or being given magic spectacles to see invisible reality. No, it is another case of catching the true significance of what has always been there to be seen. The difference is that round-earthers made their discovery out of their sharp wits and natural intelligence, whereas Christian eschatologists have learned to see by being taught of

God. But Paul stated our idea rather precisely, "When anyone is united to Christ, there is a new world; the old order has gone, and a new order has already begun" (2 Corinthians 5:17). Obviously, Paul does not mean to say that, at the moment one accepts Christ, he is transported from this world to another one. Just as obviously, that moment does not mark the disappearance of this world and its replacement by the kingdom of God. No, what *does* happen is that one "sees" the entire world (and all its people) "newly." The old, secular, flatlander interpretation is gone; and the new, true, eschatological significance has already begun.

Yet notice what follows. It is not so much that the secularist's (or flatlander's) is an utterly *false* reading of things as that his is a *partial*, or *limited*, viewpoint which, sooner or later, is bound to distort the truth. Goodness knows, there were a great many things people could and did do correctly and well, even when we were all flatlanders. Indeed, even now, as enlightened round-earthers, we still perform most of our functions under the old premises of a flat earth.

However, I would suggest, even if a true-believing flatlander and a modern round-earther were working side by side—both making the same motions and together acting as though the earth were flat—there would still be a major difference between them. The round-earther would have a true understanding of what he was doing and why. He would not be vulnerable to having his entire world-view knocked into a cocked hat by chancing upon phenomena that flatland premises cannot handle. The round-earther would be free to see whatever is to be seen rather than having to ignore the presence of that which would threaten his understanding of things. And of course, as soon as they came to matters of map-making, astronomy, long-range navigation, radio communciation, or space travel, the flatlander would be left helpless. All of which is to say that, even though secular wisdom ought not be condemned as all wrong, it cannot be accepted as all right, either.

With that, we are ready to apply this whole line of thought to our proper topic of "peace." It should be apparent that all peace-making thought, activity, and organization proceeds either from the secular premises of crusading or the eschatological premises of cross-bearing. Of course, all of the many groups and organizations that make no pretense of being anything except *secular* belong to the first category. But also, I would contend, by far the greater part of the peace teaching and activity done under church auspices belongs in this category as well. It all proceeds under the secular presupposition that war and conflict are societal malfunctions which, through the intelligent application of sociopolitical techniques, can be engineered out of the system by people of goodwill simply joining forces to lead the way.

Yet, if there is one thing our study has made clear, it is that the Bible consistently and without exception defines and describes peace in *eschatological* terms. It never speaks of peace without relating it to the activity of the horizonless God. The case is, then, that our secular-Christian peacemakers are being only superficially *biblical*. They have read their Bibles only far enough to discover that God and Jesus call for and promote "peace" and have taken this as the charter for them secularly to pursue their secular concept of peace—completely missing the fact that Scripture knows nothing of "secular peace" but has spoken exclusively of "eschatological peace" and its cross-bearing methodology.

However (and this point is all-important), we are not implying that the Bible condemns secular peacemaking as being altogether false and wrong—any more than every action undertaken out of a flatlander world view is false and wrong. At the same time, I do think biblical eschatology does imply certain judgments about secular peacemaking in general: Secular efforts can be of only limited helpfulness at best. Flatlander computations can serve well enough for traveling within a limited range; they will not serve for a journey around the world or a flight to the moon. Just so, secular peacemaking may serve in the avoiding of some wars and the resolving of some conflicts; but the Bible never suggests that secular crusades offer any hope of getting us to peace of the quality and scope it talks about.

And precisely because of its *limitations*, secular peacemaking also shows a certain instability. Even with the best of intentions, it can accidentally go demonic or become counterproductive (as with Captain Ahab). This is because its only guarantee is undependable *human* benevolence and wisdom rather than the totally dependable benevolence and wisdom *of God*. Specifically, it often becomes apparent that the motive power behind much of secular, anti-war crusading is "rage" (righteous indignation). Indeed, in many of its aspects, ours might well be characterized as "the age of rage." Secular crusades encourage such "justifiable rage" and undertake to direct it to the ends of peace and justice. But biblical eschatology knows how treacherous rage can be; its Suffering Servant is a model of how rage is to be absorbed and dampened rather than vented and used.

Similarly, secular peacemaking always is susceptible to infiltration by *violence*, that which is totally counterproductive and diametrically opposed to the avowed purpose. Often groups defend themselves against this accusation by defining "violence" solely in terms of physical brutality against persons. But if, as we proposed earlier, violence is accurately defined to include any and all activity that "violates" the dignity and God-image of others, then it becomes apparent just how many violent peace efforts there have been. It is readily understandable how this happens to secular causes: Suffering-servanthood, depending, as it does, upon eschatological possibilities of resurrection, simply does not commend itself as a *secular* technique; it does not show all that much promise of *working*. And so, as soon as it becomes apparent that suffering-servanthood is *not* working, any secular program is as much as *forced* to go to more "powerful" means. Secular peacemaking, by nature, always is susceptible to infiltration by violence.

With this, we need again to emphasize that what we have said here does *not* amount to a flat-out dismissal or condemnation of all secular peace efforts. But what, then, *should* be the Christian's attitude and relationship to these efforts? Let's try some suggestions (in order of priority).

(1) Surely the Christian's first responsibility is to *discover* the biblical, eschatological, cross-bearing view of peace—then to learn it, ground himself in it, commit himself to it, and practice it.

(2) His next obligation—and the greatest contribution he can make to world peace—is to help others make his own discovery. First, perhaps, he can help fellow Christians discover the peace-eschatology of their own gospel. But, beyond that, he also is to be an *evangelist*. It should go without saying that the gospel he represents is the gospel of peace (there being no other gospel). But we will say it anyhow: to become a Christian should be identical with becoming an eschatological peacemaker, and our evangelism should present the matter so.

(3) Although recognizing both, the Christian dare never *confuse* eschatological and secular peacemaking, cross-bearing and crusading. Above all, he dare not fall into the world's way of thinking that what secularism calls "peace" is the only peace there can be and secular methods the only means of getting there. In short, whatever the Christian may do in supporting secular peace efforts, he dare never forget that he has seen (and can see) beyond the horizon to a much greater and truer vision.

(4) Yet, at the same time, in this superior vision, the round-earther will never scorn or belittle the peace efforts of flatlanders. After all, if he *has* seen further, it is not because he is smarter or better than they but because of what God, in his grace, has given. The Christian's first desire, of course, is that flatlanders come to share his vision. But failing that (or better, while waiting for that to happen) he will have the utmost respect for the flatlanders in their peacemaking desires and intentions. He will recognize that there is true good that *can* be accomplished by them, in their way. He will recognize that it is infinitely better for flatlanders to be working for peace (even in their imperfect way) than to be working at conflict and war.

(5) Even so, the Christian will never peg his own hope for

peace upon secular efforts. May God use and bless those efforts, indeed; but his own hope is built on nothing less than the Suffering Servant's righteousness.

(6) The Christian will always give first priority to his distinctive eschatological vision, with its understanding that peace comes as people take up the ballerina role, turn to God and learn of him—or, as Isaiah put it at the conclusion of his "nation shall not lift sword against nation" oracle: "Come, let us walk in the light of the Lord" (see p. 67 above).

(7) But then, as a lesser priority, the Christian is free to cooperate with and involve himself in the sociopolitical activism of secular peace movements—as the church itself is free to engage in peace activity of a quite secular nature.

I just now was very careful to say "free to" and not "obligated to"; the distinction is vital. There may be Christians who are especially called and gifted by God to contribute in the arena of secular activism. Yet whether a person is a Christian peacemaker or not is never to be measured by the degree of such involvement. And the activist must keep aware that the fellow Christian who has chosen to pass up activism in favor of witnessing to the biblical peace-eschatology and winning people for it may be making an even truer contribution to peace than is the activist himself. But above all, secular activism dare never be proffered as a *substitute* for the Christian's and the church's primary witness. It is not its social activism that makes a peace church a peace *church*.

(8) Thus, *Christian* involvement in *secular* peace activity will call for a very discriminating stance. Yes, we have said it is right that round-earthers regularly find themselves behaving as though they thought the earth were flat—and just so should it be in flatland peacemaking. However, we also said that even when a round-earther and a flatlander are doing *the same thing*—even when they are doing it *together*—they are not actually doing *the same thing*. It is not as it appears, that the round-earther has deserted his own perspective and joined the flatlander in his. Not

at all; the round-earther remains keenly aware that his under-standing is different, yet he has discovered that the freedom is his to join the flatlander in many actions that do not violate round-earth truth. Yet, of course, the round-earther will want to stay very alert *not* to violate the eschatological truth that has been commit-ted to him.

So, especially while joining the flatlanders and working with them, the Christian will need constantly to remind himself that he is not one of them (in the world but not of it). He will, of course, be ready and eager for opportunities to witness to his own larger vision and horizonless perspective—although he will never do this by trying to force round-earth standards onto flatlanders (until they catch the vision for themselves, they are not capable of the risks of cross-bearing). Yet an important aspect of the Christian's witness will be to maintain as much of a critique toward his peace-making flatlander companions as toward the warmaking flat-landers. His biblical vision will make him especially sensitive to the entrance of treacherous rage and subtle violence. And when he sees them, he will be obligated to speak up, even at the cost of losing influence or being ostracized.

Indeed, as a cross-bearer among the crusaders, the Christian always will have to "sit loose" in any secular peace movement. Because he knows that its premises are not his, his commitment can never be fully to those efforts; his ultimate loyalty already has been pledged elsewhere. So, just as he found the Christian freedom (and calling) to come in, so must he keep himself ready to use that same freedom to get out when his Christian commit-ment calls for that. It is by his round-earth vision that he lives and dies; and his flatlander involvement always must be regulated ac-cordingly. Whether he is in or out, God's will for his life is being done. The tragedy is never that he has to leave a given peace or-ganization. No, the tragedy comes only when Christians fail to realize that they *are* different from flatlanders and have vastly greater resources to offer, when they get so caught up in flatlander enthusiasm (even peace enthusiasm) that they forget their eschatological geography. And it can happen. Sad to say, it happens all the time.

But consider that any believer is not only a Christian but is also, quite apart from his faith, a member of society and citizen of the state as well. Particularly in a democracy, this means that he has some very real obligations and opportunities having to do with the character and direction of the society to which he belongs. Thus the Christian *does* have social and political responsibilities.

And yet, when he steps into the political arena, he must realize that he is on the same footing with every other citizen: his round-earth faith does not affect his flatland competence, gives him no special leading, grants him no special wisdom, confers upon him no special status, results in no special privileges, carries no special advantages. His Bible gives him no more political guidance than it gives guidance in modern physics to the fellow Christian in the laboratory. His being a Christian affords him no more expertise in his field than it does the physicist in his. The gospel shows no more affinity for societal engineering than it does for electrical engineering. Secular politics is not a field that carries unique Christian responsibility or significance.

What does this mean? What implications follow?

I think there are several. Primarily, a Christian must be *modest* in all his plans and actions aimed at societal change. "Modesty" here includes a number of different ideas.

In the first place, the Christian will be modest regarding the hopes and expectations he places in his socio-political efforts. Political action does not touch the deep sources of man's life; it does not, for example, speak to the problem of war's "wherefrom" that Genesis treats. Thus, at best, social reorganization may accomplish some limited, partial, temporary gains for the welfare of mankind—and these, of course, are well worth working for. But if our study of the Bible has been anywhere close to the mark, it is clear that the Christian hope for man and the world far transcends and works in a different direction from human wisdom promul-

gating programs of social change. The Bible gives us no grounds
for believing that our efforts will have the effect of "turning this
country around," "greening America," or making it "Christian."
The expectations of the Christian social activist should be of about
the same order as those of the Christian physicist: he may be able
to do some good, but the salvation of humanity depends upon
God rather than upon our effectiveness.

Also, the Christian will be very modest about claiming that
his political activity is "Christian" in character, suggesting that
others ought to recognize and support it as such. The temptation
to come on "like God" is very strong in this regard. It is a question
not so much of ends as of means. Captain Ahab's end purpose in
desiring to rid the world of a monster was, of course, entirely good
and "Christian." But whether this was the proper job for *him* to
undertake and whether he went about it in the proper way—that
is where the matter became highly questionable. Just so, our study
has made it plain that Christianity is opposed to wars and fightings. However, it does not follow that anything done in opposition
to war is thereby right and good; our study also has shown that
the Bible is as particular about the *means* to peace as it is about
the fact that peace is the goal.

As we have seen, the Bible opts for the way of the suffering
servant as being *the* means to peace. As we also have seen, this
way is eminently *non*political in character. That is to say, it *is*
political in the sense that suffering-servanthood *can* have real effect upon the body politic, even though it is not calculated as a
technique for manipulating social change (Jesus' cross, for example, did revolutionize the social scene). Yet such eschatological
activity is so totally different from what the secular world knows as
"politics" that it dare not be put into the same category (there is
no way to recommend Jesus' cross as having been *politically
smart*).

Now undoubtedly there is much political activity for peace
which, judged simply under its own standards as political activity,
is contributive, helpful, and appropriate—and which can be

judged so on purely secular grounds. Yet even though it is quite
acceptable, one should be very cautious about denominating it
"Christian"—any more than our Christian physicist will call one
of his lab methods a Christian technique. To name an activity
Christian implies that it has the sanction of Scripture, is derived
directly from its eschatological vision, and has that about it which
should commend it particularly to the community *of faith*. But
the gospel is not all that clear on matters of political method.
Surely, there are all sorts of things that can be deemed "good,"
without feeling it at all necessary to go ahead and call them
"Christian."

At best, political action will be a tricky business for the Christian, because the secular game was not set up with him in mind.
The normal rules and procedures all have been designed by and
for the advantage of eastward-facing, go-it-alone Nimrodians and
not God's ballerinas. The name of the game is "power"—most
frequently "over-others power"—which is not the distinctly
Christian way. And defenseless love—which is the distinctively
Christian way—does not work politically.

Perhaps "does not work *well* politically" would be the more
accurate way of putting it; sometimes the situation does seem to
work out that nonviolent methods (which are not necessarily the
same thing as Christianity's suffering love) do prove to be
politically expedient. Nevertheless, it has to be said that political
reality is so constructed that defenseless love just is not a very re-
liable or promising technique for effecting social change. Yet, at
the same time, it should be recognized that some of the deepest
social changes in history have occurred as Christians made their
martyr-witness *without any thought or intent of being political
about it*. What it comes to, then, is that the Christian way works
when and how God chooses to work it but not as a calculated, self-
operative political technique.

Finally, the "modesty" of a Christian's political action will lie
in its being done out of motives of *serving* his fellowman rather
than attempting to put an end to evil and turn things around. The

distinction is not always an easy one to make, but it is, I believe, a valid and helpful one.

The Bible, of course, gives us ample authorization and instruction regarding "service." After all, as has been pointed out often enough, "the suffering *servant*" is the very term that identifies the Christian model; servanthood is central to our entire biblical theme. On the other hand, a call to go out, twist the tails of the monsters, and make the world shape up—this has not been part of the biblical picture at all.

How, then, does service-motivated politics differ from its contrary? No one can deny that it would be a *service* to get the way of the world redirected. It would be a service to everyone to get an armed conflict terminated, to cut down military expenditures, to prevent or conclude any program of conscription.

The difference is perhaps summed up in our word "modest." Service politics is characterized by the selection of modest, realistically attainable goals. Most of the action will be on the local level where individuals can have some real effect. There will be a short, immediate chain of consequences between the political action and the benefits envisioned for those being served.

Thus, Captain Ahab's proper service would have been to procure and deliver whale oil for the lamps of New England. This he could have done with every expectation of success; he would have as much as put the oil into the hands of the householders whose needs were to be served by it. This would be a very humble service, to be sure, but a very real one. On the other hand, his crusade to rid the world of a monster may have been heroic (or seemed so), but it also was grandiose, presumptuous, and ill-conceived. As a consequence, there was no service accomplished; a grave disservice was rendered to his men and employers; and the service he could and should have performed was thereby thwarted.

Similarly, a campaign to get a government grant for low-cost housing in the community might stand a real chance of success. The campaign itself would be the next thing to helping a needy family move into an adequate home. This would be a humble and modest service, it is true, yet a very real one. But to raid a draft office in hopes of ending a war? It is a heroic act (or so it seems), but how much different from Ahab's?

The long and short of it is that, because the Bible rather clearly chooses not to include political action as part of the distinctively *Christian* calling, it would seem wise for Christians to consider it as part of their *civil* calling, the calling they share with—and on the same footing as—all of their fellow citizens, Christian and non-Christian. Consequently, they will want to keep their political activity subordinate to their distinctively eschatological calling and be most "modest" in the use of political means.

As a way then of summing up the absence of what we didn't find in the Bible (or, what we found not to be in the Bible) and of getting us back to what we *did* find there, we present an analogy.

Christians beyond doubt are called to minister to the world—but in a particular way. The world has a bellyful of poison, or perhaps *is* a belly full of poison. The poison stems from man's choice to desert his ballerina role and go it alone, *like God;* and certainly a major part of the resultant pain takes the form of wars and fightings.

Two different ways of approaching the problem present themselves. Let us say that the poison has created the condition of "acid stomach." The *antacid* approach, then, is one obvious possibility. The action here, notice, is directed specifically against the poison; the goal is to *counteract* it, *overcome* it by superior chemical force, *neutralize* the acid with an alkali. The poison is "manipulated" so as to deprive it of potency.

Regarding the struggle for peace, this method clearly qualifies under what we have termed "political action," i.e., it is an effort to counteract evil by direct manipulation of the institutions and practices which are deemed evil. However, we have suggested that the political (antacid) approach carries with it some inherent risks and difficulties.

A manipulative effort, any attempt to counter power with power, must work from the assumption that the manipulator is wiser, stronger, and more righteous than the poison he assaults. Antacid *can* neutralize acid upset, but the matter calls for fine discrimination: go too far and the medicine becomes a poison of its own sort (which may be just what has happened in a number of anti-war efforts). Politics is a delicate operation, because it amounts to an attempt to beat evil at its own game.

But whereas the antacid approach is that of the secular world—although indubitably one that will need to be used in some degree by Christians in virtue of their also being "in the world"—there is a second approach which we propose as distinctly Christian. And it avoids some of the risks of the other method.

The second treatment for bellyache is an *emetic* designed to cause vomiting. Consider that in this case the "medicine" does not even try to act upon the poison; it makes no effort at counteracting, overcoming, neutralizing, or manipulating. The emetic's only assignment is to be what it is—*and adamantly refuse to become anything else* (the rock in the whirlpool again). It accurately can be said that an emetic does not "work" at all; it only refuses to be worked upon.

The consequence of taking an emetic is that the stomach is thrown into the convulsion (revolution) of vomiting; but in a very real sense this is not the emetic's doing. All in the world it does is refuse to be assimilated; it remains the "indigestibility" it is. The stomach actually brings convulsion on itself through its effort at making this foreign substance conform to its gastric terms. Truly, it is by "ignoring" both the poison and the stomach that the emetic has its curative effect of getting the poison disgorged.

Medically, emetic represents a much more drastic treatment than does antacid (and thus is not as often prescribed). Just so, the Christian approach of defenseless nonconformity is more radical than what usually passes as radicalism today, namely, the administering of massive doses of antacid (with very little evidence of anything like a lasting cure).

Here, then, is the sense in which defenseless love gains the victory that overcomes the world and purges it of evil. True—yes, very true—the emetic gets itself vomited out along with the poison (this is the way of the cross); but for the Christian emetic there is a resurrection that puts it back into business.

So let the draftee who has received greetings from King Jesus fight his own war in his own way (correction: "fight God's Holy War in God's holy way"). He's got nothing to lose but his life. Yet "there is no greater love than this, that a man should lay down his life for his friends" (John 15:13). "But if a man will let himself be lost for my sake, that man is safe" (Luke 9:24). How, "safe"? Because King Jesus already has been there; and "on that cross he despoiled the cosmic powers and authorities, and boldly made a spectacle of them, leading them as captives in his triumphal procession" (Colossians 2:15).

"May the Lord of peace himself give you peace at all times and in all ways. The Lord be with you all" (2 Thessalonians 3:16).

Index of Scripture Cited

OLD TESTAMENT

NEW TESTAMENT

www.ingramcontent.com/pod-product-compliance
Lightning Source LLC
Chambersburg PA
CBHW060337100426

42812CB00003B/1028